50
SIMPLE
THINGS
YOU CAN
DO TO
SAVE THE
EARTH

The EarthWorks Group

Earthworks Press
Berkeley, CA

This is dedicated to the not-yet-born.

**THIS BOOK IS PRINTED ON RECYCLED PAPER,
WITH RECYCLED INK.**

Created and Packaged by Javnarama
Designed by Javnarama

ISBN 0 - 929 - 634 - 06 - 3
First Edition 10 9 8 7 6 5 4 3 2 1

We've provided a great deal of information about
practices and products in our book. In most cases,
we've relied on advice, recommendations, and research
by others whose judgments we consider accurate and
free from bias. However, we can't and don't guarantee
the results. This book offers you a start.
The responsibility for using it
ultimately rests with you.

For ordering information, write to
Earthworks Press, Box 25,
1400 Shattuck Avenue,
Berkeley, CA 94709
or call (415)-841-5866.
Bulk rates are available.

Distributor to the Book Trade: Publishers Group West
Printed by Delta Lithograph Co.

ACKNOWLEDGMENTS

The Earthworks Group would like to thank everyone who worked with us to make this book possible, including:

- John Javna
- Julie Bennett
- Fritz Springmeyer
- Phil Catalfo
- Robin Dellabough
- Jayne Walker
- Moira A. Hughes
- Chris Calwell
- The NRDC
- Michael Brunsfeld
- Rob Pawlack
- The Ecology Center
- Karina Lutz, *Home Energy* magazine
- Kathleen Kennedy
- Marc Ledbetter, American Council for an Energy-Efficient Economy
- Pamela Lichtman, Center for Marine Conservation
- Eric Lefcowitz
- Jeanne Byrne
- Environmental Action
- Dean Roberts and Walter Bischoff, Greenleaf
- Andy Sohn
- Susan Fassberg
- Joe Pryborowski
- Dick Bunnell
- Debra Lynn Dadd
- Joel Makower
- 5th St. Computer Services

- Gene Brissie
- Peter Beren
- Jay Feldman, National Coalition Against the Misuse of Pesticides
- Larry Weingarten
- The Massachusetts Aububon Society
- Renew America
- Worldwatch Institute
- The Texas Water Development Board
- P G &E
- EBMUD
- Frances Flanigan, Alliance for the Chesapeake Bay
- Marine World Africa USA
- The Environmental Defense Fund
- Citizens for a Better Environment
- Bio-Integral Resource Center
- The San Francisco Recycling Program
- The Aluminum Assn.
- American Paper Institute, Recycling Committee
- Rich Block, World Wildlife Fund
- National Wildlife Federation

"Nobody made a greater mistake than he who did nothing because he could only do a little."

—**Edmund Burke**

Supermarket facts: Commercial kitchen cleanser is available without chlorine.

CONTENTS

Introduction...6

WHAT'S HAPPENING
The Greenhouse Effect......................................9
Air Pollution..10
Ozone Depletion...11
Hazardous Waste 12
Acid Rain..13
Vanishing Wildlife...14
Groundwater Pollution...................................15
All That Garbage 16
Saving Energy and Water,
    Saving the Earth..17

50 THINGS TO DO

SIMPLE THINGS
1. Stop Junk Mail 20
2. Snip Six-pack Rings 21
3. Use a Clean Detergent................................22
4. Aerate Your Faucet 23
5 New Ingredients 24
6. Tanks, But No Tanks...................................25
7. Make a Phone Call......................................26
8. Brush Up on Paint 27
9. Time to Re-Tire? 28
10. Home on the Range 30
11. Don't Go with the Flow 32
12. Gas Station Ecology...................................33
13. The Twilight Ozone.....................................34
14. Your Gas Is as Good as Mine 36
15. Recharge Your Batteries.............................38
16. Attention Shoppers!...................................39
17. Find the Hidden Toxics 40
18. Leave It A Lawn 42
19. Stamp Out Styrofoam................................44

INTRODUCTION

At least once a week, I get a call at NRDC from members and concerned citizens asking what they can do, personally, to combat specific environmental problems. I enjoy that part of the job, helping people get involved.

So I consult my bookshelf and then point them in a few promising directions. By necessity, the information I give out comes from a diverse array of sources, some easy, some difficult to obtain. No one has ever taken the time to compile it in one place, until now.

The Earthworks Group has given us the solution to this problem in 96 pages—a volume deceptively slim for the amount of information it contains. Want to know the facts about energy-efficient shower heads and lightbulbs, and where to buy them? It's all here. What can actually be recycled? That's here, too. Even cars, cans, tires, trash, and toilets get their moment in the sun.

Like few books in this decade have ever done, *50 Simple Things* empowers the individual to get up and *do something* about global environmental problems. No point in letting the news reports and magazine coverage drive you to despair; even the most "intractable" environmental problems march toward a solution when everyday people get involved.

Few of us can do anything to keep million-barrel oil tankers on course through pristine waters. All of us can do something, every day, to insure that fewer such tankers are needed. None of us can close the hole in the ozone layer above Antarctica. All of us can help prevent its spread to populated areas by reducing our use of chlorofluorocarbons (CFCs).

Most of the 50 Things covered here are unbelievably easy. They are the kind of things you would do anyway to save money—if you knew how much you could save. Now you do; the Earthworks Group has done your legwork for you. At the very least, this book shows you how to use energy more intelligently. Don't shiver in the dark; just make sure you're getting as much comfort and

20. It's a Beach 45
21. Buyer Beware 46
22. Pests & Pets 47
23. Make It a Royal Flush 48
24. Air-Power Your Shower 50
25. Recycle Motor Oil 52
26. Tune Up the Heat 54
27. Light Right 56
28. Don't Let Go 58

IT TAKES SOME EFFORT

29. Reuse Old News 60
30. Recycle Glass 62
31. Don't Can Your Aluminum 64
32. Precycle 66
33. Use Cloth Diapers 68
34. Put It To Work...At Work 70
35. Recycle the Rest 72
36. Build a Backyard Wildlife Refuge 73
37. Help Protect the Rainforests 74
38. The Great Escape 76
39. Plant a Tree 78
40. Prevent Pests Naturally 80
41. What a Waste! 82
42. Carpool to Work 84

FOR THE COMMITTED

43. Start Composting 86
44. Install a Graywater Tank 88
45. Drive Less 89
46. Eat Low on the Food Chain 90
47. Start a Recycling Program 92
48. Xeriscape 93
49. Stay Involved 94
50. Spread the Word 96

convenience as possible from every dollar you spend on electricity, natural gas, and gasoline.

The 1990s are bringing, I think, a new sense of awareness that institutions alone can never solve the problems that cumulate from the seemingly inconsequential actions of millions of individuals. My trash, your use of inefficient cars, someone else's water use—all make the planet less livable for the children of today and tomorrow. But remember: as much as we are the root of the problem, we are also the genesis of its solution. Go to it!

Chris Calwell,
Energy Program / Atmospheric Protection Initiative
Natural Resources Defense Council (NRDC)
—September 21, 1989

WHAT'S

HAPPENING

THE GREENHOUSE EFFECT

THE GOOD

"The greenhouse effect, when functioning normally, keeps our planet warm. Natural gases in the atmosphere form a blanket which allows sunlight to reach the earth's surface, but prevents heat from escaping (much like the glass in a greenhouse). This gas blanket traps heat close to the surface, and warms the atmosphere."

—*Global Warming: The Greenhouse Effect*
Friends of the Earth

THE BAD

"For the first time in history, human activities are altering the climate of our entire planet. In less than two centuries, humans have increased the total amount of carbon dioxide in the atmosphere by 25% from the burning of fossil fuels and the destruction of forests . . .Unless we reduce emissions of greenhouse gases, the stable, hospitable climate on which civilization is based could become a thingof the past."

— *Cooling the Greenhouse*,
NRDC

THE UGLY

The Greenhouse Gases:

• *Carbon Dioxide* (CO_2). Responsible for about 50% of the greenhouse effect. Every year, people add 6 billion tons of it to the atmosphere (1.5 billion from the U.S.). Main sources of CO_2: Burning fossil fuels such as coal, oil, and natural gas, and the destruction of forests—which release CO_2 when they're burned or cut down.

• *Chlorofluorocarbons* (CFCs). Not only responsible for 15-20% of the global warming, but also destroy the earth's ozone layer.

• *Methane*. 18% of the greenhouse effect. Produced by cattle, rice fields, and by landfills.

• *Nitrous Oxide*. Responsible for 10%. Formed by microbes, breaking down chemical fertilizers, and by burning wood and fossil fuels.

• *Ozone*. Comes from ground-based pollution caused by motor vehicles, power plants, oil refineries.

The average American family produces about 100 lbs. of trash every week.

AIR POLLUTION

BLOWIN' IN THE WIND
"Almost twenty years after Clean Air Act passed, tens of millions of Americans still breathe dirty air. According to the Environmental Protection Agency, over 76 million people live in areas where the [clean air] standard is exceeded."
—Breathing Easier,
The World Resources Institute

WHAT IS IT?
"Ozone, the primary component of smog, is a gas formed when nitrogen oxide and hydrocarbons combine in sunlight. In the atmosphere, ozone occurs naturally as a thin layer that protects us from the sun's ultraviolet rays. But when it's formed at ground level, it's deadly."
—The Clean Air Project

WHERE DOES IT COME FROM?
"Cars, trucks, and buses…are one of the chief sources of ozone. In 1986, [an astonishing] 6.5 million tons of hydrocarbons and 8.5 million tons of nitrogen oxides were [spewed] into the air by motor vehicles.…Utilities, oil, and chemical plants, are also a large part of the problem, accounting for approximately half the hydrocarbon emissions and half the nitrogen oxide emissions in the U.S."
—Exhausting Our Future,
The Public Interest Research Groups.

SMOG ALERT
"Lung damage from ozone-polluted air is a risk faced by roughly 3 out of 5 Americans.
—Exhausting Our Future,
The Public Interest Research Groups.

"Most people don't realize that smog harms other forms of life as well as people. Ozone smog is responsible for extensive damage to pines in California and in the eastern United States.…It's also to blame for crop losses in many agricultural states."
—The Clean Air Project

Americans buy (and throw away) 500 million disposable cigarette lighters every year.

OZONE DEPLETION

UP, UP...
"High above our heads, a fragile, invisible layer of ozone shields the earth's surface against dangerous solar ultraviolet radiation. The ozone layer has been there for eons."
—The Natural Resources Defense Council

...AND AWAY
"But now man is destroying this protective shield. Chlorofluorocarbons (CFCs), halons, and other manmade chemicals are wafting up to the stratosphere, 6 to 30 miles overhead. There they break down, releasing ...atoms that destroy ozone."
—The Natural Resources Defense Council

WHAT ARE CFCs?
"CFCs are put to hundreds of uses because they are relatively nontoxic, nonflammable, and do not decompose [easily]....Because they are so stable, they will last for up to 150 years. The CFC gases rise slowly to about 25 miles where the tremendous force of the sun's ultraviolet radiation shatters the CFC, freeing the chemical element chlorine. Once freed, a single atom of chlorine destroys about 100,000 molecules of ozone before settling to the Earth's surface years later. Three percent, and perhaps up to five percent, of the global ozone layer has already been destroyed by CFCs."
—Curtis A. Moore, *International Wildlife* magazine

WHAT NEXT?
"As ozone diminishes in the upper atmosphere, the earth receives more ultraviolet radiation, which promotes skin cancers and cataracts, and depresses the human immune system....As more ultraviolet radiation penetrates the atmosphere, it will worsen these health effects, reduce crop yields and fish populations. It will affect the well-being of every person on the planet."
—*Worldwatch Paper 87,* The Worldwatch Institute

Natural alternatives: Mineral oil works well as a lubricant on door hinges.

HAZARDOUS WASTE

GROWING CONCERN
"The environmental impact of the huge amounts of hazardous wastes produced each year has been of increasing national concern....In 1983, 266 million tons of hazardous waste were generated—more than a ton for every person in the United States."

—*Wrapped in Plastics*,
Environmental Action Foundation

WASTE NOT...
" Advanced nations manufacture some 70,000 different chemicals, most of which have not been thoroughly tested....Careless use and disposal of these substances contaminate our food, water, and air, and seriously threaten... the ecosystems on which we depend."

—*Citizen's Guide to Global Issues*
Coalition for a Global Tomorrow

HASTE MAKES WASTE
"Chemicals have become an indispensable part of our daily lives. We enjoy the convenience of such chemically-derived products as plastics, detergents, and aerosols, and yet we are often unaware of the hidden price tag associated with them. Eventually they find their way into water and / or the ground via landfills, drains, or sewage sludge.

—*Guide to Hazardous Household Products*,
The Clean Water Action Project

IT COMES BACK TO US
"Although consumers rarely make the connection between the everyday plastics products and packaging they buy and the growing problem of toxic pollution, many of the chemicals used in the production and processing of plastics are highly toxic...In an EPA ranking of the 20 chemicals whose production generates the most total hazardous waste, five of the top six are chemicals commonly used by the plastics industry."

—*Wrapped in Plastics*,
Environmental Action Foundation

3 million cars are abandoned in the U.S. every year.

ACID RAIN

HOW DO WE GET IT?
"Sulfur and nitrogen oxides, pollutants released by coal-burning electric-power plants or motor vehicles, are spewed into the atmosphere. There they are changed chemically ...and they fall back to Earth as acidified rain or snow. This destroys plant and animal life in streams, damages forests, and even erodes buildings."
—*Cleaning Up the Outdoors*

DROPPING ACID
The effect is staggering. Along the Appalachian Mountain chain, rain is 10 times more acidic than nearby lower elevations...and about 100 times greater than unpolluted rain. The most acidic rain measured at several eastern mountains is 2,000 times worse than unpolluted rain water. In fact, it is so acidic that it approximates lemon juice.
—*Breathing Easier,*
The World Resources Institute

DON'T JUST SIT THERE
"[We must take] action... soon, for otherwise no forest—not even in the wildernesses of North America—will be safe in the future....If we continue this pollution at the present rate, there will be scarcely any trees left to worry about in only a few decades."
—**John Seymour and Herbert Girardet,** *Blueprint for a Green Planet*

HIGHLY CHARGED ARGUMENT
" Sulfur dioxide (SO_2) is the primary [component of acid rain] in most regions, and electric utilities are responsible for approximately 65% of the total SO_2 emissions in the U.S. Therefore, large reductions in electric utility SO_2 emissions [are necessary] Electricity conservation is one [way to achieve this]."
—**American Council for an Energy-Efficient Economy**

An estimated 14 billion lbs. of trash are dumped into the sea every year.

VANISHING WILDLIFE

URBAN SPRAWL
"In 1980 there were 4.4 billion people on Earth. In 1990, there will be 5.2 billion. Every day, some of these human beings move into places on the planet where only plants and animals used to live. Forests are cut down. Wetlands, oceans, ice caps, and prairies are invaded."
—*Russell Train,*
World Wildlife Fund, U.S.

GOING, GOING...
"Extinctions are accelerating worldwide. Our planet is now losing up to three species per day. That figure is predicted to be three species per hour in scarcely a decade. By the year 2000, 20% of all Earth's species could be lost forever."
—**The Nature Conservancy**

...GONE
"Nearly all of Africa's elephants will be gone in 20 years if the present killing rate continues."
—*Defenders* **magazine**

DEAD DUCKS
"To judge by the dwindling population of North American ducks, the continent's wetlands—feeding and breeding grounds for many waterfowl—must be under severe stress. The U.S. Fish and Wildlife service estimates that only 66 million ducks migrated south this past fall (1988), 8 million fewer than in 1987."
—*Worldwatch magazine,*
Feb. 1989

EQUAL PROTECTION
"Only a few popular and charismatic mammals are receiving adequate concern and protection....It is important to fight also for less well-known species...particularly insects, fish, amphibians, reptiles, and plants. Otherwise, we will be allowing crucial pieces of the fabric that holds ecosystems together to disappear."
—**Brian Gaffney,**
The Ecology Center
Newsletter

We throw away enough iron and steel to supply all of America's automakers continuously.

GROUNDWATER POLLUTION

WATER-LOG
"As a nation, we consume 450 billion gallons of water every day. Ninety-seven percent of the Earth's supply is contained in our oceans, and 2% is frozen. We get our water from the 1% that is left, which comes from one of two places: the Earth's surface (rivers, lakes and streams) or from...groundwater."
> —**The National Coalition Against Pesticide Use**

PRECIOUS RESOURCE
"Today nearly 117 million citizens—over one-half of the U.S. population—rely on groundwater for their source of drinking water....It is no wonder that the discovery of groundwater contamination in every state across the country has generated great concern."
> *Velma Smith,*
> **Environmental Action**

WHERE DOES IT COME FROM?
"Groundwater...is water that fills the cracks and pore spaces in rocks and sediments... beneath the surface of the earth. Most groundwater is naturally pure....In many cases, groundwater remains undisturbed for years, even centuries, before it is used.... More than 90% of the world's total supply of drinkable water is groundwater...."
> —**The Water Pollution Control Federation**

THE PROBLEM
"Because we have not understood...groundwater—or how vulnerable it is—we have been careless. Gasoline or other harmful liquids have been allowed to leak from underground storage tanks into the groundwater supply. Pollutants seep...from poorly constructed landfills or septic systems. Groundwater [is] polluted by runoff from fertilized fields [and] industrial areas. Homeowners contribute to groundwater contamination by dumping household chemicals down the drain or...on the ground."
> —**The Water Pollution Control Federation**

Using a broom, not a hose, to clean driveways and steps saves hundreds of gallons of water.

ALL THAT GARBAGE

WHAT A DUMP
"More than half the cities in America will exhaust their current landfills by 1990. Already, rising mountains of trash overwhelm...town dumps, and thousands of dumps have been closed for pollution problems."
—*State of the States, 1987,*
Renew America

"America has for a long time taken the cheapest option in waste disposal: 90% of its rubbish is simply dumped in landfill sites and buried. But landfill sites are filling up; a third have closed since 1980. More than half the cities on the east coast will run out of room by 1990. In New York, 14 sites have closed in the past ten years. All of Seattle's sites will soon be full."
—*The Economist*

FLOATING GARBAGE
"No one really knows how much plastic is fouling the oceans. But a recent report ...estimated that up to 350 million pounds of packaging and fishing gear alone may be lost or dumped by fishermen and sailors each year. Millions of pounds more may come from individuals, private boats, and factories"
—**Michael Bowker,**
International Wildlife
magazine

THE WRONG PACKAGE
"The burgeoning solid waste problem reflects a trend in lifestyles...that emphasize shopping convenience, quick preparation and consumption, and easy disposal. Since 1960 the waste generated by packaging has increased more than 200%."
—**Renew America**

COMMON SENSE
" Other industrial countries produce half as much trash per person as we do, and recycle a major portion of it.... The cheapest and safest ways to deal with trash are those that make common sense: producing less waste and recycling more."
—**1988-89 *Annual Report,***
The Environmental
Defense Fund

More than 200 million tons of pesticides are used annually in California alone.

SAVING ENERGY AND WATER, SAVING THE EARTH

by Karina Lutz, Managing Editor of *Home Energy* magazine

"Energy efficiency is about getting the same, or better, services from less energy by substituting ingenuity for brute force."
—Christopher Flavin and Alan B. Durning

After living through the 1970s, we're all familiar with the sensible home economics and good foreign policy of saving energy. Take insulation, for example. The argument goes: If we insulate our homes, we'll help keep OPEC at bay. Plus, we'll save so much money on utility bills that we'll recoup our investments in a year or two...and pocket the change thereafter. Not a bad argument.

But it doesn't take the environment into account. As a result, many Americans have no idea whether saving energy—or water—makes an ecological difference. Will a dab of caulk around your drafty windows really have any effect on our shattered environment? The answer is a resounding yes.

• If you burn less oil, coal, or wood, there will be less carbon dioxide and other greenhouse gases emitted into the atmosphere, and global warming will be slowed.

• If less coal needs to be burned at an electric power plant, there will be less acid rain, less strip mining, and less air pollution.

• If less electricity is needed, there will be less nuclear waste, less uranium tailings left exposed at mines, less power plants to be built and irradiated, and less chance of future Chernobyls.

• Less gasoline burned means less smog and greenhouse gases.

• Less oil extracted from the earth means less disruption of wildlife for drilling, less offshore oil drilling, and less chance for disastrous oil spills.

About 75% of the water we use in our homes is used in the bathroom.

Similarly, saving water isn't just something to do in a drought, when the resource is scarce. Every drop of water wasted is a drop less of a wild and scenic river, a drop less of a salmon run, a drop more in a dam filling a glorious valley.

Water conservation also reduces the amount of chemicals and energy used in water treatment and sewage treatment. It reduces the amount of energy needed to pump the water to your home or heat the water once it's there. And since water heating is generally the second largest energy user in the home, that's no small potatoes.

That's not to demean the smaller potatoes. In terms of what you can do to save the earth, small savings are certainly beautiful. The Herculean task of shifting our lifestyles back into balance with the earth is no longer overwhelming when broken down into the manageable pieces of influence each of us has in our personal lives. The compact fluorescent light bulb, the low-flow shower head, the energy-efficient appliance all represent conscious—and valuable—efforts to reduce the impact that human beings will have on the world. And, in fact, the small changes we have made in the last 15 years have already had a considerable impact on the amount of energy the United States consumes.

When the first energy crisis struck in 1973, even the most ambitious predictions—that we might reduce growth to a 20% increase in our national utility bill—assumed that we would have to completely reorder society to accomplish that modest goal. By 1987, we were using 44% less energy than we would have if we kept frittering it away at the rate we'd grown accustomed to. And we did it without harsh measures—no frigid indoor temperatures, abandonment of the automobile, switching off TVs.

Conservation, it turns out, does not mean "freezing in the dark," as Ronald Reagan once said. Conservation can be accomplished by simple, cost-effective measures that require little change in lifestyle. For people concerned with saving the Earth, that is good news, indeed.

For information about Home Energy *magazine, write 2124 Kittredge St., #95, Berkeley, CA 94704.*

That's hot: The average annual energy bill for America's hot tubs is $200 million.

SIMPLE

THINGS

1. STOP
JUNK MAIL

The junk mail Americans receive in one day could produce enough energy to heat 250,000 homes.

BACKGROUND. We don't usually think of junk mail as an environmental hazard—just a nuisance. But if you saved up all the unwanted paper you'll receive in the mail this year, you'd have the equivalent of 1-1/2 trees. And so would each of your neighbors. And that adds up to about 100 million trees every year.

DID YOU KNOW
• Americans receive almost *2 million tons* of junk mail every year.

• About 44% of the junk mail is never even opened or read.

• Nonetheless, the average American still spends 8 full months of his or her life just opening junk mail.

• Junk mail is made possible by U.S. Postal Service policies that enable bulk mailers to send presorted batches of mail for their minimum rate—10.1¢ per piece.

• If only 100,000 people stopped their junk mail, we could save about 150,000 trees every year. If a million people did, we could save some 1.5 million trees.

SIMPLE THINGS TO DO
• **Write to: Mail Preference Service, Direct Marketing Association,** 11 West 42nd St. PO Box 3861, New York, NY 10163-3861. They'll stop your name from being sold to most large mailing list companies. This will reduce your junk mail up to 75%.

• **Recycle the junk mail you already get:** If it's printed on newsprint, toss it in with the newspapers. If it's quality paper, make a separate pile for it—many recycling centers accept both white and colored paper. Envelopes are recyclable, too—as long as they don't have plastic windows in them.

Packaging Mania: About 75% of America's glass is used for packaging.

2. SNIP SIX-PACK RINGS

*During a beach cleanup along 300 miles of Texas
shoreline in 1988, 15,600 plastic six-pack
rings were found in 3 hours.*

BACKGROUND. Plastic six-pack holders—the rings used for canned beer, soft drinks, oil, etc.—have become an ocean hazard to birds and other marine life.

How do they get into the water? They're left on the beach by careless sunlovers and wash into the ocean; or they're dumped into our waterways along with tons of other garbage, and gradually make their way into the oceans; or they're dumped into seaside landfills and erosion or wind propels them into the water. Once they're floating in the sea, they're hazards to marine life.

DID YOU KNOW

• Six-pack holders are virtually invisible underwater, so marine animals can't avoid them

• Gulls and terns—birds that frequent recreational areas and dumps near the ocean—sometimes catch one loop around their necks while fishing. Then they snag another loop on a stationary object. Result: they drown or strangle themselves.

• Pelicans catch fish by plunging into the water. Occasionally, one will dive straight into a six-pack ring. Result: the bird ends up with the ring stuck around its bill; unable to open its mouth, it starves to death.

•Young seals and sea lions get the rings caught around their necks. As they grow, the rings get tighter, and, the animals suffocate. Some states now require six-pack rings to be photodegradable—which means they break down in sunlight after 30 days—but that doesn't deal with the short-term problems.

SIMPLE THINGS TO DO

• Before you toss six-pack holders into the garbage, snip each circle with a scissors.

•When you're on the beach, pick up any six-pack rings you find and take them with you. Snip (or snap) them before you throw them away

The average U.S. home uses the energy equivalent of 1,253 gallons of oil every year.

3. USE A CLEAN DETERGENT

Over half the phosphates in our lakes and streams come from detergents.

BACKGROUND. Phosphates, chemical compounds containing phosphorus, are found in most detergents. Manufacturers use them because they soften water and prevent dirt particles from being redeposited on clothes.

Unfortunately, there are severe ecological side-effects: As phosphates empty into streams and lakes, they cause "algae bloom"— i.e., they fertilize algae to the point where it grows out of control. When the algae dies (in its natural cycle), the bacteria that cause it to decay—a process requiring huge amounts of oxygen—use up the oxygen needed by other plants and marine life to survive. The result: Lakes and streams can die.

DETERGENT DATA
• You may be using a high-phosphate detergent without realizing it. Look on the side of your detergent box. It will list the amount of phosphorus "in the form of phosphates." But that's not the phosphate content; to get the actual amount, multiply the percentage of phosphorus by 3. For example: 8% phosphorus = 24% phosphates.

• Phosphates aren't necessary. Many powdered detergents are made with different formulas—less that 0.5% phosphates for areas where phosphate use is regulated, and higher percentages where it isn't.

SIMPLE THINGS TO DO
• **Use a little less detergent.** According to *Consumer Reports* magazine, manufacturers recommend more detergent than necessary.

• **Use a low-phosphate, or phosphate-free detergent.** Liquid detergents are generally phosphate-free.

• **Use a substitute.** If your water is soft, soap powder will work as well as a detergent. If your water is hard, you can try a combination of soap and washing soda. But don't try it until you get more details. Send a SASE to: The Ecology Center, 2530 San Pablo Ave., Berkeley, CA 94702. Ask for their detergent fact sheet.

In the U.S., about 70% of all metal is used just once...and is then discarded.

4. AERATE YOUR FAUCETS

According to stats in Home Energy *magazine, we would save over
250 million gallons of water every day if every American
home installed faucet aerators*

B ACKGROUND. There's a simple device you can attach to the water faucets in your home that will save an amazing amount of water. It's called a "low-flow faucet aerator."

FAUCET FACTS
• The normal faucet flow is about 3-5 gallons of water per minute (gpm). By attaching a low-flow faucet aerator, you can reduce the flow by 50%. Incredibly, although the flow is reduced, it will seem stronger because air is mixed into the water as it leaves the tap.

• Installing low-flow aerators on kitchen and bathroom sink faucets will save hot water. It will also cut water use by as much as 280 gallons per month for a typical family of 4. That's over 3300 gallons a year for one family....So if only 10,000 4-member families install low-flow aerators, we'll still save over 33 million gallons a year.

• Don't confuse low-flow faucet aerators with standard screen aerators (which do not reduce faucet flow rate). Ask your store clerk if you're unsure.

SIMPLE THINGS TO DO
Installing an aerator is easy—even if you're all thumbs. The ends of most modern faucets unscrew; and that's where the aerator attaches. If you have questions, ask a plumber or local hardware store. They'll help you.

• **Portable Dishwasher Alert:** If you use a *portable* dishwasher in your kitchen, don't install a low-flow aerator on the kitchen sink faucet; the reduced flow will affect the dishwasher's performance.

SOURCES
Low-flow faucet aerators sell for less than $4 at hardware and plumbing stores everywhere.

99.5% of all the fresh water on Earth is in icecaps and glaciers.

5. NEW INGREDIENTS

If just 25% of American homes used 10 fewer plastic bags a month, we'd save over 2.5 BILLION bags a year.

BACKGROUND. The kitchen is a good place to start integrating an environmental consciousness into your every day life. By substituting environmentally sound kitchen products and practices for unsound ones, you can help conserve resources ...and play a part in changing America's habits. Some alternative products may cost more, because—at the moment, anyway—the demand is low. But as more of us buy them, prices will drop.

DID YOU KNOW
• Your coffee filters, paper towels, etc. are white because they're bleached. But this isn't a benign aesthetic; the process of bleaching paper is responsible for creating dioxin, a deadly toxic which has been dumped into American waterways.

• In many cases, paper is bleached despite the fact we rarely look at it. For example: Americans buy billions of bleached coffee filters every year, and then throw them away after one use.

• To make plastic wrap cling, manufacturers add "plasticizers," potentially harmful chemicals that can work their way into your food.

SIMPLE THINGS TO DO
• **Use reusable containers** to store food in your refrigerator instead of habitually wrapping food in aluminum foil or plastic wrap.

• **Use unbleached coffee filters.** Check your local supermarket, or contact Rockline, Inc., P.O. Box 1007, Sheboygan, WI 53082. Another alternative: reusable cotton coffee filters.

• **Keep rags in the kitchen** to wipe up spills instead of using paper towels every time. Then wash and reuse them.

• **Use biodegradable wax paper** to wrap sandwiches instead of foil or plastic. Or, for sandwich and freezer bag addicts: Biodegradable, non-toxic bags made of 100% cellulose. Write to Earth Care Co. Box 3335, Madison, WI 53704. (608) 256-5522.

Note: A variety of kitchen products are also available by mail from Seventh Generation, 10 Farrell St., South Burlington, VT 05403.

Appliances, heating, and cooling cost the average U.S. home over $1000 a year in energy.

6. TANKS, BUT NO TANKS

*Water heaters account for about 20% of all
the energy we use in our homes*

BACKGROUND. You probably don't pay much attention
to your water heater; it just sits in a dark corner gathering
cobwebs. But maybe you should. After all, it's the second-
largest energy-user in the American home.

DID YOU KNOW
• Many people keep their water heaters at 140°—hotter than necessary. Not only does that waste energy by overheating water, but
adds to heat loss in the tank and shortens its life.

• For every 10° you turn down your water heater, you save 6% of
the energy used.

• Some experts suggest keeping water heaters at 120°. But this may
pose a health risk. Bacteria that causes Legionnaire's Disease can
live in hot water heaters; 120° may not be hot enough to kill it.

SIMPLE THINGS TO DO
• Turn your water heater down to 130°—hot enough to kill bacteria and still save energy. Or put it on an "energy conservation" setting—most modern heaters have them. Note: If you have a dishwasher without a backup heater, you may have to stay with 140°.

• Insulate your water heater with a pre-fab "blanket" (available at
most hardware stores), making sure not to block off air vents (on
gas heaters). This step's important if it's in an unheated space, like
a basement. You can save 7-8% of the energy you've been using.

• Every 2 months, drain about 2 quarts of water from the valve faucet located at the bottom of the tank. This helps prevent accumu-
lation of sediment and improves efficiency and life of the heater.

SOURCES
Larry Weingarten, Elemental Enterprises, PO Box 928, Monte-
rey, CA 93942. (408)-394-7077. *Possibly America's #1 authority on
water heaters. He'll share his knowledge.*

A trigger nozzle on your hose will save at least 20 gallons when you wash your car.

7.MAKE A PHONE CALL

Let your fingers do the walking...

BACKGROUND. This may be cheating a little bit—it doesn't effect the environment directly—but when you get started on a project as important as this, it's good to know what assistance is available. As the head of one organization told us, "What's the use of getting people excited about saving cans and bottle for recycling, if they don't know where to take them?"

We think that's a good point, so we encourage you to do a little research on your own. Familiarize yourself with some of the subjects we'll be dealing with in the book, and check them out locally. You may be surprised at the diversity of services available. For example:

Call Your Local Electric Utility:
• Check on availability of energy audits.
• Ask about free information (conservation booklets, etc.).

Call Your Local Water Utility:
• Check to see what water conservation devices (low-flow shower heads, faucet aerators, etc.), services, or information they offer.

Call your Local Recycling Center
• How do you find it? Look it up in the Yellow Pages; get the information from your local city government; or call 1-800-CALL EDF and ask the Environmental Defense Fund for assistance in locating the nearest center.
• Ask what materials they collect, whether they have curbside pickups (and what days), or whether you need to bring the materials in, where the nearest drop-off centers are, etc. (see pp. 60-65).

Check out the Yellow pages; see what's listed under :
• Recycling,
• Environmental agencies (or groups)
• Car Pool (or Van Pool)
• Diaper Services
• Heating Services
• Plumbing / Electrical Supplies, etc.

The production of meats, dairy products, and eggs account

8. BRUSH UP ON PAINT

*Americans use 3 million gallons of paint every day. That's
over a billion gallons every year—enough to fill a lake
20 feet deep, 4 miles long, and 1 mile wide.*

B ACKGROUND. Everyone faces a painting decision some-
time. The decision should be more than just color,
though—what kind of paint you use, and what you do with
it when you're done, has a direct impact on the environment. In
fact, even cleaning your paintbrushes has an impact.

DID YOU KNOW
• According to the San Francisco Household Hazardous Waste
Facility, paint and paint products account for 60% of the hazardous
waste dumped by individuals. This includes oil-based paint,
thinners, solvents, stains, and finishes. Pigment in oil-based paint is
often made with heavy metals like cadmium and titanium dioxide.

• Not only is oil-based paint toxic, but the by-products of manufacturing it are also nasty pollutants. When titanium dioxide is used,
for example, liquid waste containing sulfuric acid, heavy metals,
and chlorinated hydrocarbons is generated.

• Disposing of any paint by pouring it onto the ground is risking
groundwater contamination. And letting any oil-based paint products evaporate pollutes the atmosphere; keep the lids on tight.

SIMPLE THINGS TO DO
• **Use latex paint** instead of oil-based paint.

• **Dispose of excess paint properly.** For oil-based paint: See "Hazardous Waste" on p. 82. Latex paint: Let it evaporate outdoors,
then dispose of the remaining solid waste with normal garbage.
This isn't a "quick fix"—evaporation could take up to a year.

• **Clean paintbrushes safely** (latex paint). Don't wash them outside—the paint will threaten groundwater. If you're on a sewer system, rinse them in a sink; the waste will go to a treatment facility.

• **Participate in a community "Paint Exchange."** Why let your
left-over paint go to waste, when someone else could use it?
Another alternative: Donate extra paint to a school.

for 1/3 of the raw materials used for *all* purposes in the United States.

9. TIME TO RE-TIRE?

*Every two weeks, Americans wear almost 50 million pounds
of rubber off their tires. That's enough to make
3-1/4 million new tires from scratch.*

BACKGROUND. Tires have a bigger impact on the environment than you might think. By maintaining them properly, you help conserve the energy and resources that would go into making new ones, prevent the pollution generated by tire production, save gasoline, and reduce the problems created when we throw them away. (They're bulky, don't decompose, and provide places for mosquitoes to breed.)

TIRE TRIVIA
• Some 240-260 million tires are discarded annually in the U.S. In fact, right now there are billions of tires clogging landfill space all over the country.

• Some landfill operators don't even accept scrap tires…or they charge more because tires often don't stay buried—they trap gas and float to the top of landfills.

• In New York state alone, tires take up an estimated half-million cubic yards of landfill space each year.

• It takes half a barrel of crude oil to produce the rubber in *one* truck tire.

THE COST OF INFLATION
• We don't normally think of tire inflation as an environmental issue, but it is. Keeping tires properly inflated preserves the life of the tires (preventing premature wear from "overflexing" and overheating), and saves gas.

• Right now, there are more than half a billion tires being used in the U.S. It is estimated that an incredible 50% to 80% of them are underinflated.

• Since underinflation can waste up to 5% of a car's fuel by increasing "rolling resistance," this means that more than 65 million car owners could substantially boost their cars' fuel efficiency by simply putting more air in their tires. How much gas could we save with this simple step? Up to 2 billion gallons a year.

Annually, America produces the equivalent of 10 lbs. of plastic for every person on earth.

THE RADIAL DIFFERENCE

• Radial tires really do improve gas mileage. Steel-belted tires are generally the most efficient.

• If all cars in the U.S. were equipped with the most efficient tires possible, the fuel savings would equal 400,000 barrels of oil *per day*.

RECYCLING TIRES

• Tire recycling is still a fairly untapped area. But it's a promising one. The energy used to produce a pound of virgin rubber is 15,700 BTUs. Producing one pound of recycled rubber requires only 4,600 BTUs—a savings of 71%.

• Recycled rubber can be used for tires, adhesives, wire and pipe insulation, brake linings, conveyor belts, carpet padding, lawn mower and tractor tires, hoses, sporting goods, and many other products.

• Ground rubber "crumbs" can be added to asphalt for paving roads, runways, playgrounds and running tracks. Rubber added to asphalt will increase pavement life by 4 or 5 times, and reduce the amount of resurfacing materials required.

• Most tires produced today contain less than 10% recycled rubber, which could easily be increased to 30%.

SIMPLE THINGS TO DO

• Buy the longest-lasting, most fuel-efficient tires possible. Ask your tire dealer about the "rolling resistance" and the mileage performance of the tires you're considering buying.

• Make sure your tires are properly inflated, balanced, and (every 6-8,000 miles) rotated.

• If you have a choice between tire dealers offering roughly equal prices, and one recycles, patronize the recycler. At least, ask what the dealer does with old tires; if they're not recycled, see if it's possible in your area to take them to a tire recycling center.

• Support local and regional efforts to recycle tires, to use more recycled rubber in tires, and to convert discarded tires into energy.

SOURCES

Tire Industry Safety Council, P.O. Box 1801, Washington, DC 20013. *Offers a $2.75 "glove compartment tire safety and mileage kit." It includes an air pressure gauge, a tread-depth gauge, four tire valve caps, and a 12-page "Consumer Tire Guide."*

At the rate we're generating garbage, we need 500 new dumps every year.

10. HOME ON THE RANGE

America's refrigerators consume 7% of the nation's total electricity— the equivalent of more than 50% of the power generated by all of our nuclear power plants.

BACKGROUND. Energy specialists repeatedly stress that we can have a significant impact on the environment simply by properly maintaining major appliances like refrigerators, stoves, air-conditioners, etc.

That's easy to say—but most of us don't know how.

Here are a few examples of the simple ways you can save with your appliances. But there's lots more to learn. Write to the American Council for an Energy-Efficient Economy (see Sources) for info.

DID YOU KNOW

• If all consumers raised the settings of their air conditioners by 6 degrees, we could save 190,000 barrels of oil every day.

• More than 25% of the average city apartment dweller's electrical costs go for refrigerators.

• Washing machines use about 14% of the water consumed in the home.

• Microwave ovens use only 1/3 to 1/2 as much energy as conventional ovens. Toaster ovens are more energy-efficient, too.

STOVE / OVEN TIPS

• If you're buying a gas stove: An electronic ignition system will use about 40% less gas than a pilot light

• The pilot light and burner should be burning with a blue cone-shaped flame. If it's yellow, burners and ports are clogged or need adjustment. Pipe-cleaners work well for unclogging the gas ports.

AIR-CONDITIONING TIPS

• Don't switch your air conditioner to a colder setting when you turn it on. It won't cool the room any faster and *will* waste energy.

• Clean or replace the filters once a month. Otherwise the fan has to work harder and consumes more electricity.

REFRIGERATOR TIPS
• If your refrigerator and freezer are 10° colder than necessary, your energy consumption will increase up to 25%. Check the temperatures of yours: It should be between 38° and 42°; the freezer should be 0° to 5°.

• For efficient operation: Clean the condenser coils on the back or bottom of your refrigerator at least once a year. (There's a special brush you can buy, or you can just vacuum it.)

• Keep the door gasket clean to make sure the seal isn't being broken by dried-on food.

WASHER & DRYER TIPS
• You'll save a lot of water if you wait till you've got a full load of wash. Washers use 32 to 59 gallons of water for *each cycle.*

• Up to 90% of the energy used for washing clothes goes to heating the water. A warm water wash and a cold rinse will work just as well as a hot water wash and a warm rinse on nearly all clothes. (The temperature of the rinse doesn't effect cleaning.)

• Clean your dryer's lint trap after every load to keep the air circulating efficiently.

RESULTS
The American Council for an Energy-Efficient Economy estimates that if each of us increases the energy efficiency in our major appliances by 10 to 30%, we'll reduce the demand for electricity by the equivalent of 25 large power plants!

SOURCES
• As we mentioned earlier, your local electric utility is probably a good source of information on energy conservation. *Most utilities have literature dealing with the tips listed here—often in more detail— and many provide low-cost home energy audits.*

• **The American Council for an Energy-Efficient Economy,** 1001 Connecticut Avenue NW, Suite 535, Washington, D.C. 20036. *They have the most comprehensive information we've found on appliance efficiency and purchasing new appliances. Recommended heartily: Booklets entitled "The Most Energy-Efficient Appliances" and "Saving Energy and Money With Home Appliances." Each is $3.*

A pine cone stuffed with peanut butter is a good way to feed birds during the winter.

11. DON'T GO WITH THE FLOW

*You could take a long shower every day with the water
you might waste by letting the tap run while you
shave and brush your teeth.*

BACKGROUND. Even if you don't do it, you probably know someone who leaves the water running while brushing his / her teeth, shaving, or washing the dishes. As water conservation goes, that's not just a drop in the bucket. A household can save up to 20,000 gallons of water each year by getting a grip on its faucets.

DID YOU KNOW:
• A running faucet probably uses a lot more water than you think: It puts 3-5 gallons of water down the drain *every minute* it's on.

• You can easily use more than 5 gallons of water if you leave the tap running while you brush your teeth.

• Washing dishes with the tap running can use an average of 30 gallons of water.

• If you shave with the water on, you use an estimated 10-20 gallons each time.

• If you wash your car at home, using a hose, you can use up to 150 gallons of water.

SIMPLE THINGS TO DO:
Brushing your teeth: If you just wet and rinse your brush, you use only 1/2 gallon of water. *Savings: Up to 9 gallons each time you brush.*

Shaving: If you fill the basin, you use only 1 gallon of water. *Savings: Up to 14 gallons each time you shave.*

Washing dishes (by hand): If you fill a basin, you use about 5 gallons of water. *Savings: 25 gallons each time you wash dishes.*

Washing your car: If you wash it at a self-service car wash, you use 5-10 gallons. If you use a sponge and a bucket, you use 15 gallons. *Savings in each case: Over 100 gallons over water.*

Astonishing water fact: To produce one pat of butter, 100 gallons of water is required.

12. GAS STATION ECOLOGY

According to the Massachusetts Audubon Society, one gallon of gasoline can contaminate 750,000 gallons of drinking water.

BACKGROUND. Many Americans don't realize that the type of gas we choose—and the way we pump it—has an impact on the environment.

IT'S A GAS
Leaded gas is an environmental hazard. Airborne lead from vehicle exhaust causes liver, kidney, and brain damage in humans. And scientists suspect that it's responsible for damaging crops as well. According to one estimate, more than half the 450,000 tons of lead released into the air every year comes from cars.

• So who uses leaded gas? According to the EPA, about 20% of the drivers whose cars are made for unleaded gas use leaded gas anyway. This not only renders the anti-smog equipment ineffective—so more pollutants are poured into the air—but ruins their cars, too.

• Owners of pre-1976 cars often believe their vehicles must use leaded gas. The EPA says that's a myth—it's the octane rating, not the lead, that's important. The only exceptions, they note, are when the cars are carrying heavy loads or traveling at high speeds. If your car was made to use leaded premium, try a mix of half regular and half unleaded premium with a 92+ octane rating.

DON'T FUME ABOUT IT
• Butane, a component of gasoline, helps create ozone smog when it evaporates. So when you fill your gas tank, the escaping vapors are polluting the atmosphere.

• The plastic hoods you see on many gas pump nozzles are actually vapor controls. The special gas hose fits over the tank opening and sucks fumes into the underground storage tank, preventing the vapors from escaping. More and more states are requiring gas stations to install this vapor-control equipment.

• So if there's a vapor catcher, don't pull if back, and don't pull out the gas nozzle to top off the tank. That's what lets the gas vapors into the atmosphere and creates smog

Don't forget: You can wash out plastic bags and reuse them.

13. THE TWILIGHT OZONE

According to the NRDC, "Leaky auto air conditioners are the single largest source of CFC emissions to the atmosphere in the U.S."

BACKGROUND. Rectifying ozone depletion (see p. 11) is one of the greatest challenges we will ever face. The problem is immediate and severe, but it's not out of control yet. The ozone layer is still there, and we can save it.

Constructive action begins with an understanding of what's causing the depletion, and what each of us can do about it.

DID YOU KNOW

• The ozone layer is being depleted by manmade gases (chlorofluorocarbons—also called CFCs—and halons) that are found in homes and offices all over the world.

• At one time, CFCs were considered harmless. So manufacturers used them in many different products.

• They're still being used today. Freon, used as a coolant in car and residential air conditioning and refrigerators, is a CFC.

• Some types of polystyrene foam (which people often refer to as "styrofoam") are still made with CFCs. Contrary to what you might assume, CFCs aren't just released in the manufacturing process; they're also released into the atmosphere as the foam breaks or crumbles. So the "styrofoam" cooler you took to a picnic last week could be contributing to destruction of the ozone layer right now.

• For many years, CFCs were commonly used as propellants in aerosol cans. However, in 1978, the Federal government passed a law banning most of them from aerosol cans.

• Nonetheless, 10% of aerosols still use CFCs as propellants. For example: asthma medication sprays and cleaning sprays for VCRs and sewing machines. And according to NRDC, "the world's silliest use of CFCs" is canned confetti.

• Some fire extinguishers sold for the home use halons as propellants. Unfortunately, these halons will eventually attack the ozone layer, even if the fire extinguishers are never used. Why? The

L.A. residents drive 142 million miles—the distance from Earth to Mars— every single day.

ozone-depleting gases gradually leak into the atmosphere.

SIMPLE THINGS TO DO
• **Don't buy halon fire extinguishers.**

• **Avoid polystyrene foam** (see p. 44). This includes form-fitting packing materials (like the materials that protect electronics in boxes during shipping), coolers, and foam "peanuts." If you can't tell whether the foam was made with CFCs, ask. Eventually, retailers will pass on your concern to manufacturers.

• **If you're planning to use hard foam insulation, make sure there are no CFCs in it.** Non-CFC foam insulation is available. It's nearly as effective, and won't make a hole in the sky. Check out fiberglass and cellulose insulation, too.

• **Be careful with car air-conditioners.** If you feel you must have a/c, the NRDC suggests: "When your air-conditioner breaks, don't just refill it; get it fixed properly....If you don't fix the leak, the CFCs put in today just go into the air next week." The NRDC also suggests that you only patronize repair shops that use CFC recycling equipment. Otherwise, the CFCs removed from your air conditioner are allowed to evaporate into the atmosphere.

• **Don't buy aerosol cans containing CFCs** (see list below). Better yet: don't use aerosols at all. Even with substitute gases, aerosol sprays aren't benign; propane and butane, the hydrocarbons used as propellants in most aerosols today, help create smog when they interact with sunlight. Lots of products come with non-aerosol vacuum pumps. They don't need gases, and they're just as easy to use.

SAY IT DON'T SPRAY IT!
If you're still buying aerosols, always try to check the labels. Don't buy anything if the following CFCs or halons are listed: CFC-11 (Trichlorofluoromethane), CFC-12 (Dichlorodifluoromethane), CFC-113 (Trichlorotrifluoroethane), CFC-114 (Dichlorotetrafluoroethane), CFC-115 (Monochloropentafluoroethane).

SOURCES
Natural Resources Defense Council, 40 W. 20th St., New York, NY 10011. *Write for their invaluable pamphlet, "Saving the Ozone Layer: A Citizen Action Guide." It includes a handy "Stratospheric Distress Card" to carry in your wallet for checking labels in stores.*

Earth-saving tip: When you buy new appliances, go for the most energy-efficient models.

14. YOUR GAS IS AS GOOD AS MINE

There are over 140 million cars in the U.S. According to the DOT, each is driven an average of 10,000 miles annually —which means that Americans drive more than a trillion miles every year.

BACKGROUND. We all know that cars have a serious impact on the environment—but because we depend on them in our daily lives, it's unrealistic to suggest that people stop driving altogether. (See p. 89 for suggestions on driving less)

Don't despair. Even if you drive every day, there's something simple you can do to help the earth: Make sure your car is running as efficiently as possible. Getting good gas mileage isn't just a matter of economics; a fuel-efficient vehicle is actually less destructive to our planet than a gas hog.

DID YOU KNOW

• Autos and light trucks emit 20% of this country's fossil fuel carbon dioxide (CO_2)— the key ingredient in the "greenhouse effect."

• The amount of CO_2 a car emits is directly related to the amount of gas it uses. Cars give off 20 lbs. of CO_2 for every gallon of gas consumed. So a car that gets 18 mpg will emit a ton of CO_2 every 1800 miles. By comparison, a car that gets 27 mpg will emit 2/3 of a ton—33% less—in the same distance.

• Cars also cause acid rain by emitting 34% of the nitrogen oxide spewed out in the U.S. That's more than 7 million tons every year—a figure that can be reduced by burning less gasoline.

• And cars emit 27% of the hydrocarbons that cause tree-killing, lung-damaging ozone smog. Again, this is directly related to the amount of fuel consumed.

SIMPLE THINGS TO DO

• **Keep Your Car Tuned Up.** It's the easiest way to make your car more fuel efficient. A well-tuned car uses up to 9% less gasoline than a poorly tuned car. That means 9% fewer toxic emissions.

• **Keep track of your gas mileage.** So if there's a sudden drop, you can catch it and get the problem fixed quickly.

To keep your drain clean: put a handful of baking soda and 1/2 cup of vinegar

SIMPLE GAS SAVERS
• **Don't let your car idle unnecessarily.** It takes less gas to start a car than it takes to let it idle. Idling become less efficient than re-starting your car after about a minute.

• **Keep fuel filters clean.** Clogged filters use more gas.

• **Stay light.** Check to see whether you're hauling around unnecessary weight (we mean in your car). Surprisingly, an extra 100 pounds will decrease your fuel economy by more than 1%.

IF YOU'RE BUYING A NEW CAR:
• **Check the specs.** Get the latest EPA Gas Mileage Guide to check the fuel economy figures and compare specifications.

• **Keep fuel efficiency in mind.** Remember: a car that gets 26.5 mpg (the standard set for 1989 cars) will emit 20 tons less CO_2 in its lifetime than the average car on the road today. You can now buy cars (e.g., the Geo Metro) that get almost 55 mpg—and some prototypes (the Toyota AXV) have gotten up to 100 mpg.

• **Is an air conditioner really necessary?** It's an ecological disaster. In addition to directly contributing to the greenhouse effect, and to ozone depletion by leaking CFCs, an air conditioner adds to the weight of a car—so it uses extra gas even when it's not running.

• **Weigh options carefully.** Optional equipment like power steering and automatic transmissions need a lot of energy to run. Other extras like electric motor-driven windows or power brakes don't use as much, but still add to a car's weight and reduce fuel economy.

RESULTS
Little things help: For example, if only 100,000 car owners who'd neglected tuneups started getting their cars tuned up regularly, some 90 million lbs. of CO_2 could be kept out of the atmosphere every year. A million car owners (that's less than 1%—remember, there are 140 million cars in the U.S. alone) could eliminate nearly a billion lbs. of CO_2.

SOURCES
Gas Mileage Guide. Consumer Information Center, Pueblo, CO 81009. *This free, annual Dept. of Energy / EPA publication will tell you the gas mileage you can expect from each make and model of car. It even estimates what your gas bill will be.*

down the drain and cover tightly for one minute. Rinse with hot water.

15. RECHARGE YOUR BATTERIES

Americans use 2 billion disposable batteries every year—enough to run close to a billion toys with "Batteries Not Included."

BACKGROUND. It's hard to imagine that the little batteries you use in your flashlight, radio, or camera could have any effect on the environment at all. But household batteries contain heavy metals. The most prevalent is mercury, a highly toxic substance that has become a major source of contamination at some hazardous waste dumps. Another is cadmium.

Batteries that are thrown out with the garbage are taken to landfill sites, where they corrode and break apart, releasing mercury or cadmium into the soil. And batteries that are incinerated with garbage release dangerous mercury or cadmium into the air.

DID YOU KNOW
• Prolonged exposure to mercury can not only make people extremely sick, but can even affect behavior. In the 1600's hatmakers who used mercury to treat felt and fur began acting strangely. Since no one knew that the hatters were showing the effects of mercury poisoning, it was assumed they were just crazy. Hence the expression, "mad as a hatter." And Alice's Mad Hatter.

• About 50% of the mercury and 25% of the cadmium used in the U.S. goes into batteries.

• An estimated 75% of all batteries used in the U.S. are the alkaline type—which are 1% mercury.

• The average annual use of mercury in batteries exceeds the federal limits on mercury allowed in garbage by 4 times.

SIMPLE THINGS TO DO:
• Use rechargeable batteries. Although they do contain cadmium, they last much longer than alkaline batteries—thus they contribute a little less to our hazardous waste problem.

• If it's possible in your area, recycle alkaline batteries. Although not widely employed, the technology to extract mercury and other metals from batteries for reuse does exist. Support it by recycling.

About 40% of all battery sales are made during the Christmas season.

16. ATTENTION SHOPPERS!

*According to Save A Tree, it takes one 15-to-20-year-old
tree to make enough paper for only 700 grocery bags.*

B ACKGROUND. We take it for granted that every time we
go shopping, a store clerk will put our purchases in a bag.
But do we really need the billions of bags we use annually?

PAPER OR PLASTIC?

• **Plastic shopping bags** are often more convenient than paper—
but they're not degradable (even the "biodegradable" plastic bags
never completely disappear—they just break up into little pieces),
and all plastic is made from petroleum, a nonrenewable resource.

• Plastic bags often wind up in the ocean and kill marine animals
that get tangled up in them or swallow them.

• The ink used on plastic bags contains cadmium, a toxic heavy
metal. So when printed plastic bags are incinerated, heavy
metals are spewed into the air.

• **Paper Bags** are reusable and biodegradable, but don't come ecologically cheap, either. Supermarket bags, for example, are always
made from virgin paper—never recycled—because, manufacturers
say, heavy loads require the long fibers in virgin pulp.

• Check the printing on a supermarket shopping bag—it might
say "recyclable," but it won't ever say "recycled."

SIMPLE THINGS TO DO

• Paper or plastic? Think twice before taking *any* bag if your pur-
chase is small. If every American shopper took just one less bag
each month, we could save hundreds of millions of bags every year.

• Even better, bring a cloth bag when you shop. For $9, you can or-
der a large washable canvas shopping bag with "Save A Tree" on
the side. **Save A Tree, P.O. Box 862, Berkeley, CA 94701.**

• For grocery shopping, use string bags. They're easy to carry and
fold up conveniently. You get 4 grocery-sized bags for $16.95, from
Seventh Generation, 10 Farrell St., Burlington, VT 05403

In 1987, America produced over 50 billion pounds of plastic.

17. FIND THE HIDDEN TOXICS

There are more chemicals in the average American home today than there were in the average chemical laboratory 100 years ago.

B ACKGROUND. Just because you bought something at a store doesn't mean it's safe. There are a surprising amount of toxics in your home, hidden in everything from oven and drain cleaners to personal care products.

They are a hazard—not only to you and your family when they're used, but to the environment when they're first manufactured...and when they're finally disposed of.

What makes these products particularly insidious is the fact that billions of dollars are spent every year to convince us they're necessary and will enhance our lives—when in fact they're dangerous.

Happily, there are many inexpensive, easy-to-use, natural alternatives that you can substitute for common commercial chemical products. It just takes a little detective work to figure out which products you need to replace.

ELEMENTARY, MY DEAR CONSUMER
• Don't assume a product is toxic-free just because there are no toxics listed on the label. The government doesn't require manufacturers to list every ingredient if it doesn't violate "federal safety standards." Baby powder, for example, often contains asbestos. And traces of pesticides have been found in shampoos.

• Labelling a product "nontoxic" can be misleading. "Manufacturers may place the word 'nontoxic' on their label simply by meeting the federal regulatory definition," explains *Making the Switch*. "This can mean, for example, that if less than 50% of lab animals die within two weeks when being exposed to the product through ingestion or inhalation, the product can be called 'nontoxic.' "

SIMPLE THINGS TO DO
Find the Hidden Toxics:
• The easiest way is to refer to books like *The Nontoxic Home* or *Making the Switch*. Be prepared for a shock; you'll find it hard to believe there are so many toxic chemicals in your home.

Coffee Alert: According to Debra Lynn Dadd, pesticides banned in the U.S. are

Buy or make alternative products
If you use alternatives to toxics, you reduce the risk to your family and the environment. Here are a few examples, just to whet your appetite. For more details, check the sources below.

Toxic: Permanent-press clothes and no-iron bed linens. According to *The Nontoxic Home*, these are treated with formaldehyde resin, "applied in such a way that it becomes a permanent part of the fiber." The result: toxic fumes.
Alternative: Natural fibers whenever possible.

Toxic: Oven Cleaners. Contain lye.
Alternative: Sprinkle water, followed by layers of baking soda. Rub gently with very fine steel wool pads for tough spots.

Toxic: Air Fresheners. They don't actually "freshen" air—rather, they deaden your nasal passages or coat them with oil. May contain chemicals like xylene, ethanol, naphthalene, etc.
Alternative: Herbal mixtures or vinegar and lemon juice.

Toxic: Mothballs. "Made from 100% paradichlorobenzene," which is harmful to your liver and kidneys.
Alternative: Herbal products that act as repellents, cedar chips or cedar oil.

Toxic: Permanent-ink pens and markers. Contain harmful solvents like toluene, xylene, ethanol.
Alternative: Water-based markers and pens.

SOURCES
"Making the Switch: Alternatives to Using Toxic Chemicals in the Home." Send $6 to: Publication Dept., Local Government Commission, 909 12th St., Suite 205, Sacramento, CA 95814

Nontoxic and Natural, and *The Nontoxic Home*, By Debra Lynn Dadd. Cost: $11.95. Available in bookstores, or directly from the author at P.O. Box 1506, Mill Valley, CA 94942. *She also puts out a product-oriented newsletter called "The Earthwise Consumer." Write for details.*

The Household Hazardous Waste Project, Box 87, 901 South National Ave., Springfield, MO 65804. (417) 836-5777. Send $8 for their excellent book, ***The Guide to Hazardous Products Around the Home.*** *The "recipes" for most alternative products in their book have been tested by Southwest Missouri State University.*

shipped to coffee-growing countries and used on coffee that's sent back here. Drink organic.

18. LEAVE IT A LAWN

An acre of lawn needs more than 27,000 gallons of water every
week. But Americans use even more than that; we routinely
overwater our lawns by 20 to 40%.

BACKGROUND. Lawn care isn't something you normally associate with saving the Earth. But when you consider that there are an estimated 20 million acres of lawn—and some 600 trillion grass plants—in the U.S., you can see the impact that watering, fertilizing, and mowing them might have.

If you have a lawn, it's worthwhile to learn a few environmentally sound ways of taking care of it.

MOW, MOW, MOW
Some Mower Facts:
• Set your mower blades high. Don't be a victim of "golf course syndrome." Many Americans believe a healthy lawn looks like a manicured golf course; but the opposite is true. For most types of grass, the proper length is 2" to 3" high. This encourages longer, healthier roots, and provides natural shade for the ground around each plant—which enables it to retain moisture in the soil.
• Keep mower blades sharp. Dull blades tear grass (instead of cleanly cutting it), weakening the plants, and making them more susceptible to weeds and disease.

Grass Clippings:
• "Cut it high and let it lie." During dry periods, leave grass cuttings on the lawn. This works well if you keep grass long and cut small amounts each time. Cuttings will serve as a moisture-retentive mulch and a natural fertilizer.
• At other times, use grass clippings and other lawn and garden waste to make a compost pile. It will provide your garden with natural mulch and fertilizer —and help reduce contributions to your local landfill. (See p. 86)

FILL 'ER UP
• Most established lawns need about 1" of water a week, applied slowly to prevent runoff. This is considerably more effective than

shorter, more frequent sprinklings.
• How can you tell if it's an inch? Put 3 cans around the area you're sprinkling, at varying distances from the sprinkler. Check them every five minutes to see how long it takes for an inch of water to accumulate in each. Add the 3 times together, and divide by 3 to get an average. That's how long to water.

Watering Tips:
• Due to outdoor watering, water use in America increases by as much as 30% in the summer months.
• Water from sprinklers evaporates 4 -8 times faster during the heat of the day than in the early morning. Watering at night is better than midday—there's no evaporation problem—but it can cause fungus in the grass plants. Best choice: water in the morning.
• In a drought, don't waste water on grass beginning to turn brown. It's dormant and will revive after normal rainfall begins again.

ABOUT PESTICIDES
• Homeowners use up to 10 times more toxic chemicals per acre than farmers.
• The average homeowner uses 5 to 10 pounds per lawn—for a national total of some 25 to 50 million pounds! Many scientists believe these chemicals endanger the songbird population (by contaminating the worms they eat), as well as polluting groundwater.
• A green, healthy lawn is possible without chemical pesticides. (See Source below)

RESULTS
• If every lawnowner composted grass clippings, we could cut the landfill congestion by a whopping 18% during summer and spring.

• Avoiding overwatering can save about 12% of a homeowner's water use during the summer—an average of over 50 gallons a week. If 100,000 lawnowners do it, 5 million gallons are saved.

• If even 10% of lawnowners began using organic pesticides, it would remove 2.5 to 5 million pounds of toxic chemicals from the environment every year.

SOURCE
The Chemical-Free Lawn, by Warren Schultz (Rodale Press, 1989).

1/3 of the paper mills in the U.S. use waste paper exclusively.

19. STAMP OUT "STYROFOAM"

*Americans produce enough "styrofoam" cups every
year to circle the earth 436 times.*

BACKGROUND. What we think of as "styrofoam" is
actually polystyrene foam. This material is made from ben-
zene (a known carcinogen), converted to styrene, and then
injected with gases that make it a "foam" product. The gases often
used are CFCs—which "eat" ozone molecules, depleting the Earth's
vital ozone layer. The alternatives to CFCs at present aren't wonderful. One is HCFC—95% less damaging than CFCs, but still a
threat to the ozone layer. Others are pentane and butane, hydrocarbons that contribute to urban smog. So non-CFC foam merely
trades one kind of environmental problem for another.

IT'S GARBAGE
• Polystyrene foam is completely non-biodegradable; it just won't
go away. Even 500 years from now, that foam cup that held your
coffee this morning might be sitting on the Earth's surface.

• Because of its very structure—containing large amounts of air—
all "styrofoam"—regardless of how it's made—takes up a lot of
space for its weight. This means it wastes enormous amounts of precious space at already-bulging landfills.

• Polystyrene foam is deadly to marine life. It floats on ocean sur-
faces, breaks up into pellets resembling food, and is consumed.
When sea turtles, for example, eat "styrofoam," its buoyancy keeps
them from diving; it clogs their systems and they starve to death.

SIMPLE THINGS TO DO
• There is no such things as "safe" polystyrene foam. Don't use it.
Avoid foam packaging in egg cartons, disposable picnic goods, etc.

• If you eat at fast food restaurants, ask for paper cups and plates.

SOURCE
The Ecology Center, 2530 San Pablo Ave., Berkeley, CA 94702
For information on stamping out polystyrene foam, send a SASE.

Don't leave puddles of antifreeze on your garage floor—pets like the sweet taste of the toxic.

20. IT'S A BEACH

A U.S. Fish and Wildllfe survey of albatross babies found
90% with plastic in their digestive systems.

BACKGROUND. Our oceans provide most of the planet's oxygen, moisture, and weather patterns. As the Oceanic Society says, "Without healthy oceans, life as we know it would end"—yet we've treated them as if they were expendable.

You can't save the ocean by yourself...but you *can* get involved, help focus attention on the problem, and clean up a little part of the planet that needs some loving care. You can adopt a beach.

DID YOU KNOW
• Every year on September 23, the Center for Marine Conservation sponsors a nationwide 3-hour beach clean-up.

• It's remarkably effective. In 1987, in Texas alone, volunteers collected: 31,773 plastic bags, 30,295 plastic bottles, 15, 631 plastic six-pack rings, 28,540 plastic lids, and 1,914 disposable diapers.

• Around the nation, the volunteer clean-up crew picked up a total of 2 million pounds of debris...in 3 hours!

• Taking plastic off the beach saves lives. Plastic fishing gear, bags, and other plastic waste kill up to a million seabirds, 100,000 sea mammals, and countless fish each year—and it's getting worse.

SIMPLE THINGS TO DO
• Next time you go to the beach, bring a trash bag. Then spend a few minutes picking up any litter you find.

• Join the National Beach Clean-up. Call the Center for Marine Conservation (below) for information on how to organize a group at your local beach. They'll provide standardized data cards and beach clean-up guides. You have to provide the commitment.

SOURCES
• **Center for Marine Conservation**, 1725 DeSales St. NW, Washington, D.C. 20036. (202) 429-5609.

• **The Oceanic Society**, 218 D St. SE,, Washington, DC, 20003. (202) 328-0098.

Americans spend $6 billion on their lawns every year.

21. BUYER BEWARE

80% of all ivory is taken from elephants that are illegally hunted and killed—and 30% of it is bought by Americans.

BACKGROUND. This is a short page on a huge subject. Today, a staggering 10% of all species of life on Earth are endangered. In the quest for more profits, we're even threatening cherished creatures like elephants and dolphins. As a consumer, your purchases are your power. Use it to protect wildlife.

DID YOU KNOW
• Ten years ago, there were 1.5 million elephants in Africa. Today—largely because they're being slaughtered for ivory—there are only 750,000. The elephant may become extinct by the year 2000.
• More than 6.5 million dolphins have needlessly been killed by tuna fisherman. Using circular "purse seine" nets, up to 3/4 miles long, the fishermen surround an entire school of tuna, then draw the net closed at the bottom and pull it aboard. Anything caught in the nets dies. Dolphins, which travel with yellowfin tuna, are being hauled in and slaughtered en masse.

SIMPLE THINGS TO DO
• Don't buy ivory—not for any reason, under any circumstances; don't buy tortoiseshell, coral, reptile skins, cat pelts, or other products from endangered animals or plants.
• Substitute albacore and bonita for the tuna you normally buy. (Earth Island Institute urges consumers to " keep it simple" by boycotting all kinds of canned tuna). Boycotts work: Recently, Iceland gave up some whaling as a result of a boycott of its fish.

SOURCES
Contact these groups to find out what else you can do:
• **World Wildlife Fund,** 1250 24th St. NW, Washington, D.C. 20037.
• **Center for Marine Conservation,** 1725 DeSales St. NW, Washington, D.C. 20036. (202) 429-5609.
• **Earth Island Institute Dolphin Project,** 300 Broadway #28, San Francisco, CA 94133 (415) 788-3666.

How much garbage will you generate in your lifetime? About 600 times your adult weight.

22. PESTS & PETS

There are over 100 million dogs and cats in America.

BACKGROUND. Of course, you don't want your dogs or cats to have fleas; but you don't want them to wear dangerous pesticides around their necks, either—especially since manufacturing and disposing of these products can threaten the environment, and create long term health risks for all of us. Fortunately, there are effective alternatives.

DID YOU KNOW
• The sheer numbers of flea collars used and thrown away every year—an estimated 50 million—make them a potent force.

• The pesticide on some flea collars finds its effectiveness in permanent nerve damage. The pet absorbs the chemical into its system until its tissue reeks of the toxin, and paralyzes the bugs.

• Chemicals found in pet collars include: Piperomylbutoxide (prolonged exposure can cause liver damage), DDVP (dichlorvos, which, according to *Harrowsmith* magazine, "can cause cancer, nerve damage and mutations in animals"), and carbaryl (which "may cause birth defects in dogs").

FLEE, FLEAS
Some flea-collar alternatives:
• You can order citrus-oil sprays or make your own. Run orange or grapefruit skins through a food blender or processor, then simmer with some water. After the pulp is cooled, brush into your pet's fur with your hands. Remember to use only skins, as fruit juice will make the fur too sticky.

• Try adding brewer's yeast and garlic to your pet's food. For some reason, the fleas hate it.

• Look for products containing methoprene, a growth inhibitor "that interferes with flea larvae development."

SOURCES
The Bio-Integral Resource Center, P.O. Box 7414, Berkeley, CA 94707. *Check out their publications on "Least Toxic Pest Management for Fleas."*

Dispose of smoke detectors carefully: Some have radioactive parts.

23. MAKE IT A ROYAL FLUSH

*40% of the pure water you use in your house is
flushed down the toilet.*

BACKGROUND. Your toilet probably uses more water
than necessary. But with a one-time, ten-minute invest-
ment, you can save water every time you flush.

TOILET TALK
• Each time your toilet is flushed, it uses 5 to 7 gallons of water.
But if you've got a toilet tank, you can easily cut that amount by
15% to 40%

• The cheapest and simplest way: install a "displacement device," which reduces the amount of water your tank will hold.

• A displacement device can cut your annual water use by thousands of gallons—and you'll never notice it's there.

• Don't use a brick as a displacement device. Small pieces can
break off and damage your plumbing system.

SIMPLE THINGS TO DO
Put a Plastic Bottle In Your Toilet Tank:
• Small juice bottles, dishwashing soap bottles, or laundry soap
bottles work well.

• Soak off the label, fill the bottle with water, put on the cap, and
place it in the tank. To weight it down, you can put a few stones in
the bottom of the bottle.

• Be careful that the bottle doesn't interfere with the flushing
mechanism.

• You may need to experiment with bottle sizes. Different toilets
need different amounts of water to maintain proper pressure for an
effective flush.

Savings: 1-2 gallons per flush.

Leaves alone can account for 75% of the solid waste stream in the autumn.

...Or Put a Displacement Bag in Your Tank:

• These bags are specifically designed to displace toilet tank water. You just fill one with water and hang it on the inside of the tank.

• It may take some experimenting to figure out how full to fill it. Again, the amount of water you can displace without affecting performance depends on the toilet.

• They're available free from some utilities—or at plumbing supply and hardware stores (they're cheap).
Savings: 1-2 gallons per flush.

...Or Install Toilet Dams:

• These devices artificially make your tank smaller. They're "plastic barriers that isolate part of the tank so that the water in this section does not run out with the flush."

• Each dam can hold back one gallon. Two dams can be installed in one toilet.

• Installation is fairly simple; the dams come with do-it-yourself instructions. They're available at hardware and plumbing stores.
Savings: One gallon per toilet dam.

RESULTS

Even with a plastic bottle, you save lots of water. If the average toilet is flushed about 8 times a day, that means a savings of 8-16 gallons every day...56-112 gallons a week...2,900-5,800 gallons a year. If only 10,000 people were to install the simplest displacement device, that would equal a savings of 29 million to 58 million gallons a year! And if 100,000 people did it...well, use your imagination.

IF YOU 'RE BUYING A NEW TOILET

According to *Home Energy* magazine: "The newest development in human waste disposal is the 'ultra low-flush' toilet, which empties the bowl with 1/2-1/1/2 gallons of pressurized water and, in some cases, compressed air, rather than a larger volume of water at atmospheric pressure. It utilizes the water pressure in the house pipes. While a conventional toilet lets water fill the tank and lose pressure, the ULF keeps it trapped at the high-line pressure until it squirts into the bowl."   Check with local plumbing supply stores for info.

Every 3 months, the U.S. throws away enough aluminum to rebuild our commercial airfleet

24. AIR-POWER YOUR SHOWER

If a family of four takes 5-minute showers each day, they will use more than 700 gallons of water every week —the equivalent of a three-year supply of drinking water for one person.

BACKGROUND. For a lot of us, a long, hot shower is a guilty pleasure—it feels great, but there's a nagging suspicion we're wasting precious water.

Here's good news: There's a simple, effective way to cut shower water use by about 50%; just replace your conventional shower head with a "low flow" model. It's a good way to save natural resources *and* cash without having to do much.

SHOWER FACTS
• Showers usually account for a whopping 32% of home water use.

• A standard shower head uses about 5-7 gallons of water per minute (gpm)—so even a 5-minute shower can consume 35 gallons!

• "Low-flow" shower heads reduce water use by 50% or more. They typically cut the flow rate to just 3 gpm—or less. So installing one is the single most effective water conservation step you can take inside your home.

• According to the Dept. of Energy, heating water is "the 2nd-largest residential energy user." With a low-flow shower head, energy use (and costs) for heating hot water for showers may drop as much as 50%

SIMPLE THINGS TO DO
First, find out if you need a low-flow shower head:
• Use the "Bucket Test" : All you need is a watch with a second hand and a bucket that holds at least a gallon.

• Turn on the water to the pressure you normally use.

• Hold the bucket just below your showerhead and measure the time it takes the water to reach the "1 Gallon" line. If it's less than 20 seconds, your shower is a candidate for a low-flow model.

If you're an average American: 1/3 of your garbage is packaging you toss out immediately.

Next, Take a Look at What's on the Market:
There are two types of low-flow showerheads:
• **Aerated:** Mixes air with water to maintain a steady spray at pressures equal or higher than a standard showerhead. The only drawback: if you're tall, you may notice that the water's cooled down a little by the time it gets to your feet. This is by far the most popular type of low-flow shower head.
•**Nonaerated:** No air is mixed into the flow. It maintains heat and gets a good, forceful spray...but the flow "pulses." If you're partial to massage showerheads, this one is for you.

RESULTS
• With a low-flow shower head, a family of four which normally takes 5-minute showers saves at least 14,000 gallons of water a year. So if only 10,000 similar families were to install low-flow shower heads, we could save around 140 million gallons. And—get this— 100,000 four-person families with low-flow shower heads could save 1.4 billion gallons!
• NDRC estimates that a good low-flow showerhead will pay for itself with energy and water savings in less than a year if your water heater uses natural gas and less than six months if it's electric.

NOTE: Don't buy "flow restrictors" (disks that insert in your existing showerhead) or cheap, plastic showerheads. Both deliver far less satisfying showers than a well-designed, low-flow model.

RESOURCES
Your local utilty may have low-flow showerheads available for free. If not, check a good hardware store. The following companies also sell a variety of efficient showerheads..

• **Ecological Water Products, Inc.**, 1341 West Main Rd., Middletown, R.I. 02840. (401) 849-4004
• **Interbath, Inc.**, 427 N. Baldwin Park Boulevard, City of Industry, CA 91746. (818) 369-1841
• **Vanderburgh Enterprises, Inc.** Box 138, Southport, CT 06490. (203) 853-4429. *If you're more interested in non-aerating showerheads, these have been recommended by some experts.*

Only 3% of the Earth's water is fresh water.

25. RECYCLE YOUR MOTOR OIL

Americans use approximately a billion gallons of motor oil every year—and 350 million gallons of it winds up in the environment.

BACKGROUND. Auto manufacturers recommend that we change the oil in our cars every 6,000 miles. But they don't tell us what to do with the old oil. It's become an important issue; used motor oil is perhaps the worst oil for the environment, because it's not just oil—while it's flowing through your engine, it picks up all kinds of extra toxins.

DID YOU KNOW

• Some experts estimate that 40% of the pollution in America's waterways is from used crankcase oil. About 2.1 million *tons* of the stuff finds its way into our rivers and streams every year.

• When used motor oil is poured into the ground, it can seep into the groundwater and contaminate drinking water supplies. A *single* quart of motor oil can pollute 250,000 gallons of drinking water.

• Pouring oil into the sewer (or onto the street, where it will eventually wash into the sewer) is like pouring it directly into a stream or a river. And just *one pint* of used motor oil can create a poisonous oil slick an acre in diameter.

• Tossing oil into the trash is essentially the same thing as pouring it out. The oil will be dumped in a landfill, where it will eventually seep into the ground.

SIMPLE THINGS TO DO

If you get your oil changed at a gas station:
• Check first to make sure they plan to recycle it. If not, take your car somewhere where they do.

If you change oil yourself (and about 50% of American drivers do), recycle it:
• Most communities have gas stations or oil-changing outlets that

It takes 1/2 a gallon of water to cook a pot of macaroni...and a gallon to wash the pot.

recycle their oil and will accept yours for a small fee, ranging fom 25¢ to $1 a quart. It costs, because they have to pay someone to pick it up. Call around to find one close to you.

• To make the whole process easier, you can invest in a do-it-yourself oil recycling kit. These come with containers that double as oil-draining receptacles and carrying cases for transporting the oil to a recycling center. We know of two of them on the market: the "Pac-Lube Oil Changer," made by Pacific Landings, Ltd., and the "Oil Change Recycling Kit," by the Scott Paper Co. If your local automotive store doesn't have them, contact the companies directly at the addresses listed below.

RESULTS:

• Most recycled oil is reprocessed and sold as fuel for ships and industrial boilers. The rest, according to our source, is processed into lubricating and industrial oils.

• Another source adds that there is a future in re-refining it into motor oil. A new technology, created by Evergreen Oil of San Francisco, can turn a gallon of used motor oil into 2.5 quarts of new oil. Compare that to the 42 (yes, 42!) gallons of virgin oil it takes to make the same 2.5 quarts. "Imagine," says one expert "—If America refined the billion gallons of motor oil we use every year, we would save 1.3 million barrels of oil every day. That's half the daily output of the Alaska Pipeline!"

RESOURCES:

Pac-Lube Oil Changer
Gary Wilson
Pacific Landings Ltd.
1208 S.W. 13th, Suite 200
Portland, OR 97205
(503) 222-2343

Scott Oil Change Recycling Tub
Scott Paper Do-It-Yourself Business
Scott Plaza
Philadelphia, PA 19113
(800) 321-2250

Just one part oil per million parts water will make drinking water smell and taste funny.

26. TUNE UP
THE HEAT

If each U.S. household lowered its average heating temperatures by
6° F. over a 24-hour period, we'd save the energy equivalent
of 500,000 barrels of oil every day.

BACKGROUND. How important is it for you to heat your home efficiently? An expert from the American Council for an Energy Efficient Economy puts it this way: "The single most important thing people can do to save energy in their homes is to make sure their furnaces are running efficiently. More energy is used for heating than for any other purpose in American apartments and houses."

FURNACE FACTS
•According to Worldwatch, home heating is responsible for spewing 350 million tons of carbon into the atmosphere every year—which means over a billion tons of the most prevalent greenhouse gas, CO_2.

• About 12% of U.S. emissions of sulfur oxide and nitrogen oxide—both key causes of acid rain—come from home heating.

• 40% of the energy you use in your home is for heat.

• If your heating system is running inefficiently, 30-50% of the energy it uses is wasted.

SIMPLE THINGS TO DO
Get a Furnace Tune-Up:
• This means testing it (for combustion efficiency and pollutants), cleaning it (e.g., dirt on the nozzle, sediment in the boiler, soot in the combustion chamber), and adjusting it (calibrating thermostats, etc.).

• Gas furnaces should be tuned every two years, oil furnaces should be tuned up annually.

• The easiest way to get a tune-up is to call a heating technician. He or she should do the whole job for around $40-$60.

• If you want to do it yourself—or just want to know more about

You can cut your heating bill by 2% for every degree you turn down your thermostat.

the process, write to the Massachusetts Aububon Society to order the superb booklet listed below. It's extremely informative.

RESULTS
• A simple tune-up can increase a furnace's heating efficiency by 5%—with a corresponding reduction in destructive emissions.
• In a gas furnace, a 5% rise in efficiency means an annual savings of 8,000 cubic feet of gas. So if 100,000 families—only a tenth of a percent of U.S. households—get tune-ups, we'll save over half a billion cubic feet a year.
• For an oil furnace: the annual savings is about 60 gallons of oil per tune-up. If only 100,000 families get tune-ups, it's a savings of about 6 million gallons.

A FEW HEATING TIPS
If You Have a Forced-Air System:
Insulate ducts wherever they pass through unheated spaces.

• During heating season, change your air filters once a month. Your heater uses more energy when they get full of dust.

• **Common myth:** Many people believe it's better to keep the furnace running at an even temperature than to lower it drastically when no one's around. Not true. Even if you go out of a room for a little while, it's better to turn down the heat.

If You Have an Electric Heating System:
Consider installing a heat pump, which "uses thermal energy from outside air for both heating and cooling." Initial cost may seem high (as much as $2,000 for a whole-house unit, about $400 for a single room), but it can cut your heating bill by 40% a year.

If You Have a Hot Water / Steam System:
Put a reflector behind your radiator (you can buy one or make it by taping aluminum foil on cardboard). This saves energy and cash by throwing back heat you'd normally lose through the wall.

SOURCES
• The best booklet we've found is called "Heating Systems." It's available from: **Public Informations Office, Massachusetts Audubon Society, Lincoln, MA 01173.** Write for info on ordering it.

An open fireplace damper can let 8% of your heat escape through the chimney!

27. LIGHT RIGHT

Every year, Americans buy over a billion incandescent lightbulbs.
That's three acres of bulbs every day.

B ACKGROUND. Flip a light switch on and off...and consider that you're affecting the environment. It may seem strange, because we're used to thinking of lighting as a domestic matter; it happens *in* our homes, not outside them. Yet according to the World Resources Institute, lighting accounts for 1/5 of all the electricity consumed in the U.S.—which means that our lighting habits and choices have a significant impact on the Earth. The more electricity we use, for example, the more industrial emissions we generate, contributing heavily to problems like the "greenhouse effect" and acid rain.

There are several simple ways to "light right." The most obvious is conservation—diligently turning lights off when they're not in use. But a less obvious—and more effective—method is to choose and use your lightbulbs with energy conservation in mind.

LIGHT READING
The Compact Fluorescent:
• Most Americans are unaware of the development of the compact fluorescent lightbulb. This amazing bulb screws into standard sockets, and gives off light that looks just like a traditional (incandescent) bulb—not like the fluorescents we're used to seeing in schools, offices, etc. The compact fluorescents with "solid state" ballasts are the best; they come on instantly and produce no flicker or hum.

• Compact fluorescents are big energy-savers. They last longer and use about 1/4 of the energy of an incandescent bulb. For example: A 60-watt incandescent bulb lasts about 750 hours; a fluorescent bulb with 1/4 the wattage will generate the same light and burn for 10,000 hours in five to ten years of normal use.

• Substituting a compact fluorescent light for a traditional bulb will keep a *half-ton* of CO_2 out of the atmosphere over the life of the bulb.

• **Money talk**: Compact fluorescents are considerably more expensive than traditional incandescents...initially (about $15). But

A "long-life" incandescent bulb is less energy-efficient than a standard bulb.

don't compare that to the cost of one incandescent bulb. You will need 13 incandescents to last for the same 10,000 hours.
• Over its lifetime, a compact fluorescent uses about $10 worth of electricity; during the same period, equivalent incandescents gobble about $40 of electricity. So you save $30 per bulb—which is like earning 25% to 50% interest on your investment.
• Compact fluorescents aren't suitable for every type of lighting situation. One factor is size; they won't work, for example, in small lamps or certain covered fixtures. Another factor is frequency of use. They make the most sense if they're used in places where they're left on for at least 2 hours a day.
• You can't get compact fluorescents everywhere; you may have to look around a bit. Check hardware and home stores.

RESULTS
• There are 100 million households in America. If a single compact fluorescent was installed in each of them, the energy equivalent of about 60 million incandescent bulbs would be saved.
• How much is that? It's the equivalent of all the energy generated by one nuclear power plant running full-time for a year.

BRIGHT IDEAS
• Interestingly, one large incandescent bulb is more efficient than two small ones in a multi-bulb fixture. A 100-watt bulb, for example, puts out as much light as two 60s...and it saves energy.
• In light fixtures that take three bulbs, try using only two. But for safety's sake, put a burned-out bulb in the last socket.
• Try more efficient incandescents such as krypton-filled, tungsten-halogen, or infrared-reflective coated.

SOURCES
Home Energy magazine. **2124 Kittredge St. #95, Berkeley, CA 94704.** *The best magazine in America on home energy. Write for subscription info; send $2 for their excellent "Consumer Guide to Energy-Saving Lights," a highly recommended first resource.*

White Electric: The Lightbulb Place, 1511 San Pablo Ave., Berkeley, CA 94702. (800) 468-2852 *outside CA;* (415) 548-2852 *in CA. Mail orders energy-saving lightbulbs, including some compact fluorescents. Send self-addressed, stamped envelope for info.*

Energy-saving tip: Keep lightbulbs clean; dirt absorbs light and uses more energy.

28. DON'T LET GO

*Balloon releases are a popular way to celebrate special events. In
one recent promotion, for example, 1.2 million helium-filled
balloons were released into the air.*

BACKGROUND. In 1985, an emaciated 17-foot female
sperm whale died on the New Jersey coast. When marine
scientists examined it, they found a balloon—with 3 feet of
ribbon still attached—blocking the valve that connected the
whale's stomach to its intestines. Because the whale had swallowed
the balloon, it was unable to digest food; it was starving.

Since then,similar incidents have been recorded—notably with
sea turtles that died after swallowing partly-deflated latex balloons.

UP, UP, AND ASTRAY
• Balloons released in the Midwest can wind up in the ocean. Recently, a test balloon released in Ohio reached the South Carolina
coast in only two days.
• When balloons land in the water, they quickly lose their color.
With ribbons or strings trailing behind them, they look uncannily
like jellyfish—which are among turtles' favorite foods.
• For some reason, schools of squid—the sperm whale's favorite
food—congregate around pieces of plastic in the water. When they
surround a latex balloon, whales will swallow that, too.
.• **Additional hazard:** As Mylar (metallic) balloons float into the
air, they can get caught in power lines and cause power outages.

LOFTY IDEAS
• If you buy helium-filled balloons, hold onto them—don't release
them into the atmosphere when you're through with them.
 • If your group plans a balloon release, inform people of the potential hazards. Most of us aren't aware that balloons pose a risk.

SOURCES
Balloons and Clowns, 703 North Milwaukee Ave., Libertyville, IL
60048. A mail order shop run by concerned balloon-ologists. Send
self-addressed, stamped envelope for info on balloon ecology.

Manufacturers' secret: Paper towels and toilet paper are often made from recycled paper.

IT TAKES

AN EFFORT

29. REUSE OLD NEWS

*It takes an entire forest—over 500,000 trees—to supply
Americans with their Sunday newspapers every week*

BACKGROUND. The entire American paper industry was actually built on recycling. Beginning in 1690—when the first U.S. paper mill was established near Philadelphia—paper was made exclusively of fiber taken from cotton and linen rags. It wasn't until the 1860s, when the growing demand for paper products created shortages, that techniques were developed to use wood fiber in papermaking. Then the composition of paper began to change rapidly.

By 1904, 60% of American paper was made with wood pulp (although 40% was still recycled rags and waste paper). But by the 1930s, paper was made primarily with virgin materials. Even during the recycling drives of World War II, the highest level of recycled material used in paper manufacturing was just 35%.

In 1988, Americans recycled about 24 of the 80 million tons we used—a 29% recovery rate. Not bad, but we can still do a lot better.

EXTRA! EXTRA!
• Americans use 50 million tons of paper annually—which means we consume more than 850 million trees That means the average American uses about 580 pounds of paper each year.

• Making new paper from "old" paper uses 30% to 55% less energy than making paper from trees; and it reduces related air pollution by 95%.

• Recycled paper could easily be substituted for virgin paper in many products without any loss of quality—but because the demand for it has been low, recycled paper prices tend to be higher than virgin stock…which, in turn, makes it harder to get. The result: Manufacturers that could use recycled paper don't bother.

SIMPLE THINGS TO DO
Newspapers are probably the easiest material to recycle, since they

The U.S. uses 450 billion gallons of water every day.

lie around the house anyway. Recycling them is a simple way to get into the recycling habit.

1. Save them
• Don't throw newspapers out with the garbage anymore.

• Sort them. Magazines, with their slick paper and coated covers, are not easily recyclable.

• Stack them. The key to a personal recycling program is to have a place in your home where the newspapers *always* go.

2. Recycle them.
Find a recycling program near you. There are lots of options:

• Curbside recycling. (Call your local city government to find out if this service is available in your community.) Note: You'll probably have to bundle and tie them.

• Drop them off in designated receptacles at supermarkets, shopping centers, etc.

• Take them to commercial recycling centers. (Look in the yellow pages.) If the market is right, they'll pay for the papers. So if you're part of an organization, consider a fundraising newspaper drive. More than $100 million is earned annually by recycling news.

RESULTS
• According to the American Paper Institute, the average American consumes about 120 lbs. of newsprint annually—the equivalent of one tree.

• So if everyone in the U.S. recycled even 1/10 of their newspapers, we would save about 25 million trees every year.

SOURCES
Paper Recycling Committee, American Paper Institute, 260 Madison Ave., New York, NY 10016. (212) 340-0600. *Fascinating pamphlets on recycling paper, available free.*

Earth Care Paper Company, PO Box 3335, Madison, WI 53704. (608) 256-5522. *Send for their recycled paper catalog to order everything from gift wrap to postcards. They also provide free handouts or will refer you to sources on organizing newspaper drives, recycling terminology, dioxin in papermaking, and packaging. Plus Earth Care donates 10% of its profits to environmental organizations.*

Recyclers: Robins, chickadees, and orioles like to use small lengths of string in their nests.

30. RECYCLE GLASS

Each year we throw away 28 billion glass bottles and jars—enough to fill the twin towers of New York's World Trade Center every two weeks.

BACKGROUND. People have been making glass for approximately 3,500 years. Most glass is made of three basic ingredients: white sand, soda, and lime.

The materials are heated to around 2,500 degrees F—until they're completely dissolved and transparent. Then the mixture is cooled to around 1,800 degrees F. The whole process takes about 7,600 BTUs of energy to produce a single pound of glass.

Before recycled glass is shipped to the manufacturers, it is broken so it will take up less volume. This broken glass is called "cullet."

When it arrives at the factory, cullet is run through a magnetic device designed to remove metal rings from bottles. A vacuum process removes plastic coatings and paper labels; then the cullet is ready to be added into the mixture.

Because cullet lowers the melting temperature of the mixture in manufacturing glass, up to 32% less energy is required. That's a huge amount—especially when you consider how much glass we produce every year.

GLASS GOSSIP

• The energy saved from recycling one glass bottle will light a 100-watt bulb for four hours.

• All glass bottles and jars can be recycled. But other types of glass, such as window panes, Pyrex, and light bulbs, are made by different processes and can't be combined with the cullet from which glass containers are made.

• Glass produced from recycled glass instead of raw material reduces related air pollution by 20%, water pollution by 50%.

• Disposable or "throwaway" bottles consume three times as much energy as reusable, returnable containers.

• Because glass takes so long to decompose, the bottle you throw away today might still be littering the landscape in the year 3,000.

Doesn't matter if a refrigerator door's open for 15 seconds or 30—cold air's escaped already.

SIMPLE THINGS TO DO
Start with basic recycling:
• The easiest way to recycle glass at home is to set up your garbage so you can separate and save bottles in a convenient way, either indoors or outdoors.

• For example: Keep a box for glass in a closet, or buy a plastic garbage pail to keep outside and store the glass in as you use it.

• Sort bottles according to color: clear, green, and brown.

• Remove any lead collars, corks, or metal caps which can't be removed magnetically. But don't worry about paper labels.

• Rinsing is sometimes suggested, but isn't absolutely necessary. (Check with your local recycling center.)

• Once you've got a place to put the bottles as you use them, it only takes about 15 minutes a week to keep up the recycling.

If you're more ambitious:
• Start a glass recycling fundraising drive for your favorite institution. There are recycling plants that pay for glass.
• Support "bottle bills," which require consumers to pay deposits on bottles, and then refund the deposits when bottles are returned. In the nine states which already have bottle bills, a 90% compliance rate reduces solid waste by 8% and reduces litter by 50%.

RESULTS
• All the glass that you turn in for recycling is actually used to make new glass.
• Using recycled glass means using up fewer natural resources. Although sand is plentiful, it still must be mined and transported, as must the lime and soda. These processes require energy and produce about 385 lbs. of mining waste for each ton of glass produced. This can be reduced by almost 80% when 50% recycled glass is used in the process.

SOURCES
Glass Packaging Institute, 1801 K St. NW, Washington, D.C. 20006. (202) 887-4850. *Offers free pamphlets on glass recycling.*

Garbage magazine, P.O. Box 56519, Boulder, CO 80322. *Actually, this superb full-color "Practical Journal for the Environment" covers everything in practical ecology. Highly recommended!*

Contrary to popular belief: Small appliances don't add much to your electric bill.

31. DON'T CAN
YOUR ALUMINUM

*When you toss out one aluminum can you waste as much energy as
if you'd filled the same can half full of gasoline and
poured it onto the ground.*

BACKGROUND. Aluminum is the most abundant metal on earth, but it was only discovered in the 1820s. At that time it was worth $1,200 a kilogram, more than gold. According to Worldwatch Institute: "Since its first use as a toy rattle for Napoleon's son, aluminum's use has escalated. The first all-aluminum beverage can appeared in 1963, and today accounts for the largest single use of aluminum.... In 1985 more than 70 billion beverage cans were used, of which almost 66 billion—or 94%—were aluminum."

YES YOU CAN-CAN
• If you throw an aluminum can out of your car window, it will still litter the Earth up to 500 years later.

• If you throw away 2 aluminum cans, you waste more energy than is used daily by each of a billion human beings in poorer lands.

• According to the Aluminum Association, Americans recycled 42.5 billion aluminum cans in 1988.

• In 1988 alone, aluminum can recycling saved more than 11 billion kilowatt hours of electricity, enough to supply the residential electric needs of New York City for six months.

• The energy saved from one recycled aluminum can will operate a television set for three hours.

• Recycling aluminum cuts related air pollution by 95%.

• Making aluminum from recycled aluminum uses 90% less energy than making aluminum from scratch.

SIMPLE THINGS TO DO
Because recycling aluminum is so profitable for manufacturing

Where does aluminum bauxite come from? Most is imported from Guinea, Australia, Brazil.

companies (they make $2 million *every day* from recycling), there probably are more different ways to recycle aluminum than any other material. Check to see which programs exist in your area:

• Multi-material drop-off centers with separate bins for aluminum.

• Buy-back operations with scales to weigh recycled aluminum and pay consumers accordingly.

• Large, igloo-like containers for aluminum only, often found in supermarket parking lots.

• Curbside pickup.

• Reverse vending machines. These machines accept aluminum cans, reject ferrous cans, glass, or other unwanted objects. They weigh or count the aluminum deposited and dispense money or tokens in payment.

Before You Recycle Your Aluminum:
• Remove food, rinse, crush, and bag or box cans.

• Remember: a lot more than cans can be recycled, including aluminum foil, pie plates, frozen food trays, window frames, and siding.

RESULTS
• According to Recycle America's statistics: If only 250 people (including you, of course) each recycled one can a day, we would save the energy equivalent of 1,750-3,500 gallons of gasoline every year. Now try that calculation with 250,000 people; just one can a day could save the energy equivalent of between 1.75 and 3.5 million gallons of gas. And *that's* only .1% of the U.S. population, with a single can apiece.

• If we recycle, we mine less raw materials. To produce one ton of aluminum from raw materials, it takes a phenomenal 8,760 pounds of bauxite and 1,020 pounds of petroleum coke. But according to Aluminum Association estimates, this figure is cut down by 95% when recycled aluminum is used.

SOURCES
The Aluminum Association, 900 19th St. N.W., Washington, D.C. 20006. *They've got lots of info on how to recycle, how to set up fundraising events, stats, etc. Most of it's free.*

The largest single source of waste paper collected for recycling is corrugated boxes.

32. PRECYCLE

One out of every $11 that Americans spend on food goes for packaging. In fact, we spent more on the packaging for our food last year than American farmers received in net income.

BACKGROUND. In 1989, the city government of Berkeley, California initiated a campaign to encourage consumers to buy food packaged in biodegradable or recyclable materials. They called it "precycling."

"We *recycle* items after we've bought them," they explained. "We can *precycle* while we shop....This may be the easiest way to help save the Earth. Simply by making the correct buying choices, by *precycling*, we can prevent excessive and unsound materials from getting into our waste stream."

"Precycling" is a wonderful term for something we can all practice; just follow the simple, sensible slogan, "Reduce waste *before* you buy!"

DID YOU KNOW
• Each American uses about 190 pounds of plastic per year—and about 60 pounds of it is packaging which we discard as soon as the package is opened.

• About 30% of all plastics produced are used for packaging.

• Americans go through 2.5 million plastic bottles every hour.

• Packaging waste accounts for approximately 1/3 of all the garbage Americans send to landfills.

• Roughly 5 million tons—more than half of all plastics we throw away each year—are packaging.

SIMPLE THINGS TO DO
Keep your eyes open when you shop. Everything you buy has an effect on the environment—try to make it a positive one.
Some examples of simple "precycling":

• Buy eggs in cardboard—not styrofoam—cartons.

• Most cereal boxes are made of recycled cardboard. It's easy to tell—the boxes are gray on the inside. The packaging for many

The smallest drip from a leaky faucet can waste over 50 gallons a day.

varieties of cookies, crackers, dry goods etc. are also recycled. Look for the "recycled" logo, or send for the "Environmental Product Shopping List" listed below.

• Buy in bulk: It's cheaper, and uses minimal packaging (in some places, you can even bring your own container).

• Buy carrots, onions, potatoes, etc. loose, and not in plastic bags.

• Buy beverages in glass or aluminum containers, which are easy to recycle. You can also choose sauces, condiments, baby foods, spreads, etc. that are packed in glass instead of plastic.

• Avoid plastic containers, especially "squeezable" ones, which are made up of different types of plastic in several layers, and are dramatically non-biodegradable.

If you want to do more:
• Teach your children to precycle. Children are particularly susceptible to loud, colorful packaging, especially on products they've seen on TV. But they're also quick learners, and have a special fondness for nature. Teach them that they can help save their Earth by using one kind of product instead of another, by caring for their toys so they won't need replacing, by getting involved, as you are, in "doing it right, from the start."

• Urge your community to adopt "precycling" measures to promote precycling awareness. (See Source below for assistance.)

RESULTS
If 10% of Americans purchased products with less plastic packaging just 10% of the time, we could eliminate some *144 million pounds* of plastic from our landfills, reduce industrial pollution, and send a message to manufacturers that we're serious about alternatives.

SOURCES
The Environmental Shopper (*a list of products that use recycled packaging, plus an instructive booklet, for $2*)
Pennsylvania Resources Council, 25 West 3rd St.,Media, PA 19063

For community information: Call the city of Berkeley, California at 415-644-8631. *They'll pass on information about their precycling campaign that may help you put one together in your area.*

A recycled aluminum can is typically re-melted and back in the store within 6 weeks.

33. USE CLOTH DIAPERS

*Americans throw away 18 billion disposable diapers a year
—enough to stretch to the moon and back seven times.*

BACKGROUND. In 1961, Proctor and Gamble introduced the first affordable disposable diaper, Pampers. To most parents, it seemed like a triumph of modern technology—a clean, convenient way to deal with an unpleasant, messy problem.

It was an instant financial bonanza for P&G, too. Other brands soon appeared, and today there are dozens of varieties to choose from. But along with them comes indisputable evidence that disposable diapers are taking a serious toll on the environment.

DIAPER DATA

• About 1% of all of America's landfill space is occupied by disposable diapers. They can take up to 500 years to decompose in a landfill. Cotton diapers, which can be reused up to 100 times, decompose in 1 to 6 months.

• Disposable diapers consume an incredible amount of resources annually in America—1,265,000 metric tons of wood pulp and 75,000 metric tons of plastic.

• Manufacturers recommend that people wash out disposable diapers before discarding them, but only about 5% of us do. This means that every year, millions of tons of soiled, potentially disease-infected diapers are dumped into "sanitary" landfills.

• Environmental Action estimates that because of disposable diapers, "3 million tons of untreated feces and urine end up in landfills rather than in the sewage system every year." The biggest potential problem: contamination of groundwater by viruses. E. A. points out: "More than 100 different intestinal viruses are known to be excreted in human feces, including polio and hepatitis." Fortunately, no groundwater contamination of this nature has been discovered. But with the build-up growing geometrically, it may be just a matter of time.

• Degradable disposable diapers don't seem to be the answer. They do decompose faster than standard disposables (they have a cornstarch base, so the plastic breaks into little pieces)—but they take up the same space in landfills, and the health risks are the same.

The world's shipping industry dumps over 450,000 plastic containers into the sea every day.

DIAPER-DOs

This is a tough one—not because there's any question about what we *ought* to do, but because it's hard to give up disposable diapers. A recent poll, for example, showed 87% of Americans prefer them.

If You're Ready for Cloth Diapers:

• Diaper services pick up and deliver cloth diapers. Find them in the Yellow Pages, or contact the National Assn. of Diaper Services, 2017 Walnut St., Philadelphia, PA 19103. (215) 569-3650.

• Cloth diapers are ecologically sound—waste disposal is monitored by municipal health boards, and worn-out diapers are recycled into rags for industry.

• Prices are competitive with disposables—in fact, they may be cheaper, depending on whose statistics you believe. Some indicate that diaper services can be half as expensive as disposable diapers.

If You Have a Hard Time Switching to Cloth Diapers:

Remember, it doesn't have to be all or nothing. Better to alternate between cloth and disposables than to use disposables exclusively.

• One possibility: Use a diaper service at home, and disposable diapers when you're away. And if your child goes to a day-care center, he or she will need disposables there, too.

If You're Using Cloth Diapers, You'll Need Diaper Covers:

Cloth diapers don't absorb moisture the way disposable diapers do, so you'll need diaper covers to act as a shield between the diaper and the rest of the world. Natural fibers are best, and 100% wool felt seems to be the top of the line because it offers "complete breathability," and doesn't irritate babies.

SOURCES

• *Mothering* magazine, P.O. Box 1690, Santa Fe, New Mexico 87504. *Best place to learn about natural-fiber diapering products.*

For diaper covers and related products:
• **Bio-Bottoms**, P.O. Box 6009, 3820 Bodega Ave., Petaluma, CA 94953. *Wool and other natural fiber products. Send $1 for catalog.*
• **Baby Bunz and Company**, P.O. Box 1717, Sebastopol, CA 95473. *Another natural fiber company. Send $1 for catalog.*
• **R. Duck Company**, 953 West Carrillo St., Santa Barbara, CA 93101. *They specialize in nylon coverings.*

Over a billion trees are used to make disposable diapers every year.

34. PUT IT TO WORK
...AT WORK

*Every year, Americans throw away enough office and writing
paper to build a wall 12 feet high, stretching from
Los Angeles to New York City.*

B ACKGROUND. Most of the things you've been working
on at home apply to work, too. It's not always easy to imple-
ment them, but it's worth it—an enormous amount of the
Earth's resources are consumed at businesses, and an enormous
amount can be saved. Added incentive: you may wind up a hero
because recycling can save your company big bucks.

DID YOU KNOW
• The average office worker throws away about 180 pounds of high-
grade recyclable paper every year.
• Each ton of recycled paper saves more than three cubic yards of
landfill space.
• Every ton of recycled office paper saves 380 gallons of oil.
• Almost 3 million tons of paper is collected from office buildings
and industrial plants for recycling.
• The Electric Power Research Institute estimates that American
businesses could easily save 50% of the electricity they use every
year. For example: By removing 2 lamps in a 4-lamp fixture and installing reflectors instead, most businesses could cut their electric
bills and never notice the difference in brightness.

SIMPLE THINGS TO DO
By yourself: It's okay to do some little things just for your own sat-
isfaction. They might not save the world, but they *will* make you
feel better and help keep you focused on conservation. For
example:
• Bring a coffee cup to work instead of using disposable cups.
• Reuse manila envelopes by putting gummed labels over the old
addresses. Any stationary store should have them.

A layer of mulch around trees will slow the evaporation of moisture.

Projects to work on with co-workers:

• **Set up glass and aluminum recycling programs.** This usually means putting containers for saving bottles and cans in a prominent place in the lunchroom, or next to soda machines.

• **Set up a special environmental bulletin board** and post notices with interesting tidbits and statistics about conservation. Include photos when appropriate.

• **Substitute paper cups** (which are biodegradable) for styrofoam cups (which aren't).

• **Set up a paper recycling program.** There's a simple procedure: Each employee saves paper at his or her desk. The trick is to sort paper into recyclable groups *as it's discarded,* by using desktop containers. Then the custodian can collect it and deposit it in large containers outdoors, with little or no extra time required. For a detailed plan, write to the San Francisco Recycling Program (below).

• **Save water at work by lobbying for faucet aerators,** low-flow shower heads, toilet water displacement gadgets—anything you've tried at home that would be applicable at work.

• **See if you can get a two-sided copy machine.** You'll save thousands of pages when copying lengthy reports.

• **Have an energy audit** to assess your use of electricity, etc. It can make a big difference: In 1989, for example, one small business in Emeryville, California saved $2,000 in energy costs by making a simple change in their lighting configuration—a trick they learned through an energy audit.

SOURCES:

San Francisco Recycling Program, 271 City Hall, S. F., CA 94102. *Offers a wonderful booklet called "Your Office Paper Recycling Guide" for $5.00. Make checks out to the City and County of San Francisco.*

Conservatree, 10 Lombard St., San Francisco, CA 94111, (415) 433-1000. *For bulk quantities of recycled colored and white bond paper, computer paper, mimeo paper, copier paper, envelopes, etc.*

Your local electric utility. *They'll help with an energy audit, and help you contact specialty companies that can help replace lighting.*

Plywood emits formaldehyde—it's one of the home's biggest indoor polluters.

35. RECYCLE THE REST

Americans produce 154 million tons of garbage every year—enough to fill the New Orleans Superdome from top to bottom, twice a day, every day. 50% of this trash is recyclable!

BACKGROUND. Although newspaper, glass, and aluminum are the most commonly recycled items, they aren't the only ones you *can* recycle. Tin cans (which are actually 99% steel), plastic soda bottles and milk cartons, telephone books and corrugated cardboard are all recyclable.

DID YOU KNOW
• We'll repeat it: In the U.S., we throw away 2.5 million plastic bottles every *hour*—and only a small percentage of are recycled.

• Recycled plastic can be used to make a number of products, such as plastic lumber and fiberfill sleeping bag insulation. Bonus value: 26 recyclable plastic soda bottles can make one polyester suit.

• Recycling and reusing the material in "tin" cans reduces related energy use by 74%; air pollution by 85%; solid waste by 95%; and water pollution by 76%....Yet only 5% of tin cans are recycled.

SIMPLE THINGS TO DO
Recycle "other" materials the way you'd handle glass, etc.
• First, check to see exactly what your local center accepts.

• If it takes plastic: Recycle plastic soda bottles, plastic wrap, water bottles, coffee can lids, six-pack neck rings, and clean milk bottles.

• If it accepts tin cans: Rinse, remove paper labels and both ends, and flatten. (This reduces the volume, and cuts shipping costs.)

• If it accepts corrugated paper, kraft paper, and stationery: They'll probably tell you to flatten cardboard and paper, separate white from colored paper, and bag or box it. If they don't accept corrugated, see if you can locate a waste paper dealer near you by looking in the yellow pages under "waste paper" or "recycling."

SOURCES
• Call the **Environmental Defense Fund Hotline,** 1-800-CALL EDF. *They'll provide information on recycling programs in your area.*

Don't forget: Your old car battery is worth money when you trade it in on a new one.

36. BUILD A BACKYARD WILDLIFE REFUGE

The American Holly tree bears fruit in the winter, providing much-needed food for over 40 different species of birds.

BACKGROUND. Helping to save and care for animals can begin in your own backyard. By landscaping and planting with wildlife in mind, you can make up for the loss of much of their natural habitat. Simply by choosing the right plants, you can provide them with natural food and shelter...and yourself with a window—literally—into the natural world.

DID YOU KNOW
• You can attract specific animals to your garden with certain plants. Hummingbirds, for example, like red morning glories; butterflies are attracted to brightly colored flowers in full sunlight.

• Animals that are active in the daytime (e.g., chipmunks, and rabbits) will visit yards if shelter such as walls and shrubs is provided.

• Birds are often desperate for water in winter, when the ground is frozen. A heated birdbath can help hundreds of birds to survive.

• You can set up a bird feeder on a city balcony as well as a country garden. Even if you have cats, there are safe ways to put up feeders.

SIMPLE THINGS TO DO
• Consult a nursery or your local chapter of the Audubon Society to find out what flowers and trees will attract the wildlife you'd like to invite into your backyard.

• Create a Plan: Sketch out your yard and decide where to plant, provide water, and provide shelter. Then send your plan (along with $5) to the National Federation of Wildlife. They'll look it over, make recommendations and certify your yard as an official Backyard Wildlife Habitat. It's a great way to involve kids.

SOURCE
National Wildlife Federation Backyard Wildlife Habitat Program. 1412 16th Street N.W., Washington, D.C. 20036-2266. *Send for info on the program, and their list of recommended books.*

Orioles love to eat oranges.

37. HELP PROTECT THE RAINFORESTS

Each year, 27 million acres of tropical rainforests are destroyed.
That's an area the size of Ohio, and translates to 74,000 acres
per day...3,000 acres per hour...50 acres per minute.

BACKGROUND. Some people consider the destruction of the world's rainforests the most frightening of all recent ecological developments, because it's something they can measure. The tropical rainforests, located in a narrow region near the equator in Africa, South and Central America, and Asia, are disappearing so fast that by the year 2000, 80% of them may be gone.

A tropical rainforest is technically defined as a forest in the tropics which receives 4 to 8 meters of rain per year. Beyond that, it is nature's laboratory for all kinds of plant, animal, and insect life. The world's tropical rainforests are critical links in the ecological chain of life that makes up the planet's biosphere.

DID YOU KNOW
• Although rain forests make up only 2% of the earth's surface, over *half* the world's wild plant, animal and insect species live there. In a typical four-mile-square patch of tropical rainforest you would find: over 750 species of trees, over 1500 different kinds of flowering plants, 125 different mammals, 400 kinds of birds, 100 reptiles, 60 amphibians, and countless insects—including 150 types of butterflies. And only 1% of these species has ever been studied!

• 80% of all Amazonian deforestation has taken place since 1980.

• One in four pharmaceuticals comes from a plant in a tropical rainforest. About 70% of plants identified by the National Cancer Institute as being useful in cancer treatment are found only in rainforests; 1,400 rainforest plants are believed to offer cures for cancer.

• Tropical rainforests produce oxygen and consume CO_2. The rainforests of Amazonia produce about 40% of the world's oxygen.

• Latin America and Southeast Asia have already lost 40% of their tropical rainforests.

• Deforestation contributes between 10 and 30% of worldwide

Every year, Americans generate about 1,200 lbs. of solid waste per person.

CO_2 emissions. In 1987, rainforest fires (one method of clearing) pumped about 518 million tons of carbon into the air, roughly 1/10 of the total world fossil fuel combustion for that year.

WHAT HAPPENS TO RAINFORESTS

• The world's rainforests are being depleted as a result of several developments: agriculture and population resettlement; beef cattle ranching; major power projects like dams, hydroelectric plants, and the roads that go with them; and logging.

• The soil in rainforests is not rich; only about a two-inch layer contains any nutrients. Most of a rainforest's nutrients are stored in the vegetation. When a rainforest is converted to, say, cattle grazing, the soil is grazed out within two years. The cattle operation must move on, but it leaves behind a desert.

WHAT YOU CAN DO

• This is more than a political cause; it's a fight to save a precious piece of the world. Who knows what may be discovered in the rainforests—an unknown plant that provides a cure for cancer? A new crop that can feed starving children? Unfortunately, the only real influence you may have is on the people who provide financial support to countries with rainforests. So we suggest you write letters expressing your concern. The Rainforest Action Network (listed below) will supply names and addresses. Write, also, to your elected representatives about the issue.

• Support organizations involved in rainforest conservation. Indians in the Amazon are trying to foster their own sustainable rainforest-based economy; their Center needs your support. The Rainforest Action Network has information on the Center.

• Consider alternatives to tropical hardwoods in furniture, lumber, and plywood. To stop importing tropical hardwoods, the U.S. would have to reduce its consumption of timber by only 2%. Write to the Rainforest Action Network for a list of woods you can substitute for tropical hardwoods.

SOURCE

The Rainforest Action Network, 301 Broadway, Suite A, San Francisco, CA 94133. (415) 398-4404. *An organization devoted exclusively to preserving the rainforest. They will supply more information about the rainforests and what you can do.*

It takes 1,630,000 gallons of water to feed an American for a year.

38. THE GREAT ESCAPE

*Every winter, the energy equivalent of all the oil that
flows through the Alaskan pipeline in a year
leaks through American windows.*

BACKGROUND. Since the energy crisis of the '70s, experts have been telling us regularly that insulating is one of the best ways to save energy. We don't want to bore you by saying it one more time, but frankly, you can't take energy conservation seriously without making sure your home is properly insulated. It isn't always simple—it can take both time and money. But the savings in energy and cash will make it worthwhile.

INSULATION FACTS
• If every gas-heated home was properly caulked and weather-stripped, the natural gas saved annually would be enough to heat about 4 million homes.

• Nearly half of all the energy used in our homes is wasted. It goes "out the window," or through the attic, cracks or other leaks, in the form of heat—or, in summer, air conditioning—lost to the outside.

• Attic insulation can save 5% or more on heating costs—15% on air conditioning costs (it depends on the climate).

• In some climates, new insulation can pay for itself in a single season! In most climates, it takes only one or two years.

SIMPLE THINGS TO DO
Insulate:
• If there's no insulation in your home, you're costing yourself and the environment a fortune. If you do have insulation, check to see if you have enough. Even add-on insulation pays itself back in about 2 years.

• The U.S. Department of Housing and Urban Development (HUD) in Washington, D.C. has a publication on insulation called "In the Bank...Or Up the Chimney."

Have an "energy audit" to find the heat leaks in your house or apartment:
• This can range from simply going around the window frames and

sashes of your house with a lighted candle (if the flame flickers, you need caulking and weatherstripping) to calling your local utility or an energy-conservation contractor (see "Energy" in the yellow pages) and having the energy audit done professionally.

• Many utilities will do this at no charge. Or, if you're going to do it yourself, they'll often provide guidebooks or checklists to help.

If You're Doing Your Own Energy Audit:

• *Worldwatch* magazine suggests: "Pick...a cold, windy day, when secret drafts and leaks reveal themselves readily to the flame of a hand-held candle. An inspection should include more than just outer walls, since chances are the innards of your house are like Swiss cheese."

• Be sure to check everywhere for energy leaks—fireplace dampers, cracks or holes in walls and ceilings, sites where plumbing or wiring penetrate walls, floors and ceilings, attic doors, etc.

• Windows also deserve special attention. Options range from high-tech windows, to simple caulking.

Check Out Blower Doors:

A recent experiment by a New England electric utility, reported in *Home Energy* magazine, revealed that contractors using a device called a "blower door" were able to reduce leaks 7 to 8 times as well as residents who tried to find the leaks themselves. So it may be worth it to find a contractor who uses one in his energy audits.

RESULTS

According to Worldwatch Institute, an average furnace uses the energy equivalent of 500 gallons of oil in a year. If, by insulating, you save a mere 5% of the energy used to heat your home (a reasonable amount), you'll save the equivalent of 25 gallons a year; 10,000 conservation-minded families will save 250,000 gallons'-worth; 100,000 families will save 2.5 million gallons...and so on.

SOURCE

• **Public Information Office, Massachusetts Audubon Society,** Lincoln, MA 01173. *Write for info on how to order their booklets, "How to Weatherize Your Home or Apartment," "All About Insulation," and "Superinsulation."*

In six months, a leaky toilet wastes 45,000 gallons of water.

39. PLANT A TREE

The average American uses the equivalent of 7 trees every year.
That's over 1-1/2 billion trees used annually in the U.S.

B ACKGROUND. Trees can, over time, remove large quantities of carbon dioxide (the main "greenhouse gas") from the atmosphere. This makes planting a tree an effective way to fight the greenhouse effect. And it's easier than you might think.

TREE TALK

• 10,000 years ago, before agriculture, more than 15 billion acres worldwide were covered by forest. Today barely 10 billion acres are forested. Between mid-century and 1980, the forested surface of the earth was reduced by roughly 25%.

• In some places deforestation is proceeding at a runaway rate. In California, urban trees are dying or being removed at four times the replacement rate. Each year, 28 million acres of tropical forest are destroyed; some countries, like Nigeria, which once were large lumber exporters, have become net importers.

• The interdependence between trees and human and animal life couldn't be more fundamental: We require oxygen and produce carbon dioxide (CO_2) ; trees and other plants require CO_2 and produce oxygen. Any significant loss in forested land directly affects the Earth's atmosphere for other forms of life.

• By consuming CO_2, trees mitigate the "greenhouse effect." It's estimated that each mature tree consumes, on average, about 13 lbs. of CO_2 per year.

• When trees in a forest die naturally or are responsibly harvested, the trees are replaced and there is no net loss of CO_2 to the atmosphere. But when a forest is burned or clearcut, much of the CO_2 is lost and not recaptured. So on balance, the forests we lose (net loss) account for about 25% of global CO_2 emissions.

• By providing shade and evaporative cooling, trees also affect local temperature—again, urban trees even more than rural ones. Clusters of urban trees can cool ambient air temperature by 10°,reducing local energy demand (for air conditioning) by 10 to

How can you find a leak in your toilet? Put some dye in the tank—if the

50%. Moreover, the energy saved reduces global warming by about 15 times the amount of CO2 absorbed by those trees.

SIMPLE THINGS TO DO
• If you'd like to plant a tree, but don't know how to begin: Call or visit a local nursery, horticultural society, arboretum or botanical garden. Tree-planting is a lot easier than you think, and many people will be not only helpful, but enthusiastic.

• Consider talking with neighbors to see if you can begin a neighborhood- or community-wide planting effort. You'll be surprised at how much "native intelligence" you can uncover.

• Don't just stick a tree in the ground and ignore it. Like other growing plants, trees need a little care for the first two years— including water, vertical support, and mulch.

RESULTS
• Planting 100 million urban trees would reduce CO2 emissions in the U.S. by 18 million tons, and energy consumption by 40 billion kilowatt-hours (worth $4 billion), annually.

• Planting trees has a cumulative effect: each tree you plant will provide benefits for years to come. For example: If only 100,000 people each plant a tree this year, the trees will still be absorbing over a million pounds of CO2 annually in the year 2010. But if the same people plant a tree *every* year from now until 2010, the trees will absorb over 20 million pounds of CO2 in that year.

SOURCES
TreePeople, 12601 Mulholland Dr., Beverly Hills, CA 90210 (213) 769-2663. *A private nonprofit that got a million trees planted in Los Angeles before the 1984 Olympics. Send $10 for their book, "A Planters' Guide to the Urban Forest."*

Worldwatch Institute, 1776 Massachusetts Ave. NW, Washington, D.C. 20036. *Their Worldwatch Paper #83, entitled "Reforesting the Earth," is an excellent overview of the challenge. Cost: $4.*

American Forestry Association, Global Releaf Program, P.O. Box 2000, Washington, D.C. 20013. (202) 667-3300. *Has a program to help plant 100 million trees by 1992.*

color shows up in the bowl without a flush, you've got a leak.

40. PREVENT PESTS NATURALLY

Many pesticides are used for cosmetic purposes only.

BACKGROUND. When DDT was introduced in the '40s, it was regarded as a miracle; after thousands of years of fighting agricultural pests, human beings had finally devised a "safe" and "effective" way to keep them at bay. With DDT, scientists believed, agricultural land would become more productive and the world's hungry could be fed.

But that's not what happened. DDT proved to be toxic not only to insects, but to all life. As Worldwatch puts it, DDT "contaminated the food chain, pushed bald eagles and other predatory birds toward extinction, and accumulated in fish, wildlife, and people."

The DDT story is an apt metaphor for all chemical pesticides. Once they seemed ideal; now the evidence is mounting that they are an ecological disaster. Although they're designed to eliminate specific "target" pests, they often poison birds and other wildlife instead. They are seeping into groundwater and contaminating drinking water. They are even destroying the soil itself by killing essential organisms, from microbes to earthworms. And they are harmful to humans—especially children.

Yet, pesticide use grows. We dump an estimated 2.7 billion pounds in the American environment every year. Homeowners spend $1 billion a year on them. Some 300 million pounds of pesticide poisons are used right around the house, often in the kitchen or bedroom.

Fortunately, there are effective natural alternatives to chemical pesticides. As consumers, we should encourage farmers to use them. And we should learn to use them around our homes.

DID YOU KNOW
• Ironically, pesticides don't seem to be improving agricultural yield; before their use, farmers lost about 33% of their crops to pests. Today, farmers still lose the same 33%.

• According to the EPA, at least 74 pesticides have been found in the groundwater of 38 states.

If you have mice in your house—a mousetrap is still the best way to catch them.

- Over 100 active pesticide ingredients are suspected to cause birth defects, cancer, and gene mutation.
- Fact of life: Sooner or later, targeted pests develop resistance to specific pesticides, rendering the chemicals worthless. More than 440 species of insects and mites, and 70 types of fungus are now resistant to pesticides.
- Home pesticides are just as lethal as agricultural ones. According to *Harrowsmith* magazine, for example: "Just five tiny granules of diazinon, among the most widely used chemicals in consumer pesticides, are enough to kill a house sparrow or a redwing blackbird."

SIMPLE THINGS YOU CAN DO
Learn about alternatives
- They work. In 1982, for example, the city of Berkeley, California, officially banned the use of herbicides and pesticides on its property. Since that time the city has successfully managed its extensive parks and gardens without toxic chemicals.
- You can do it, too. The best technique seems to be IPM— Integrated Pest Management, which focuses on using natural pest controls, such as natural predators. See source below for details.

Buy organically grown produce and grains.
- If you can't find a local store that carries organically grown food, make a special request. You're not the only one who'll be asking.
- Demanding organic food bears fruit: In California, for example, organic food production has gone from a $20 million business to a $100 million business in only 4 years—and it's still growing.

SOURCES
National Coalition Against the Misuse of Pesticides, 530 7th St. SE, Washington, D.C. 20003. *The vanguard in the fight against pesticides use. Has numerous pamphlets and articles, most for a small cost. Also publishes a newsletter entitled* Pesticides and You.

The Bio-Integral Resource Center, P.O. Box 7242, Berkeley, CA 94707. *Publishes* IPM Practitioner, *a magazine about Integral Pest Management.*

Mothers and Others. 40 West 20th St., New York, NY 10011. A project of NRDC *Publishes a newsletter called* " tlc." *Also available: a fine book called* For Our Kids' Sake ($7.95).

41.WHAT A WASTE!

In 1982 officials in Albuquerque, New Mexico determined that local residents were generating 1.6 million pounds of hazardous waste—and were dumping 90% of it into sewer systems, garbage, or the ground.

BACKGROUND. Most Americans don't know how to dispose of household hazardous wastes properly. Some of us, for example, innocently dump toxics down the drain or into the sewer system—which might be the worst possible way to get rid of them, since wastewater treatment plants aren't designed to handle hazardous materials, and the result can be serious water contamination.

Disposing of them in landfills doesn't work, either; hazardous wastes dumped into a landfill can seep into the groundwater, run off into surface water, or pollute the air.

Since there are so many hazardous products in use—and since they can have such a lethal impact on the environment—it's important for us to learn what products we have, how to store them, and what to do when we're done with them.

DID YOU KNOW

• Hazardous wastes often found around homes include: Paints and paint thinners, car batteries, oven and drain cleaners, mothballs, floor and furniture polish, brake or transmission fluid, antifreeze, rug and upholstery cleaners, pesticides, and furniture strippers. Even products used to clean toilets are considered hazardous.

• People seem to have little idea when they're dealing with hazardous wastes. According to Environmental Hazards Management: "It has been estimated that in an average city of 100,000 residents, 3.75 tons of toilet bowl cleaner, 13.75 tons of liquid household cleaners, and 3.44 tons of motor oil are discharged into city drains each month."

• How do you figure out what's a hazardous waste and what isn't? Use available reference materials. Recommended: *Hazardous Wastes from Homes.* Cost is $4.25 from Enterprise for Education, 1320A 3rd St., Suite 202, Santa Monica, CA 90401.

For a convenient "Household Hazardous Waste Wheel," send $3.75 to Environmental

SIMPLE THINGS TO DO
Store hazardous materials properly:
- Keep them in their original containers. Don't take the chance that someone might mistake and misuse them.
- Make sure labels are securely fixed to containers.
- Keep them in a cool, dry place—out of the reach of children.
- If the original container leaks, put the whole thing in a larger container...and don't forget to mark it.

Try to reduce the amount of hazardous products you use:
- Buy exactly what you need. Remember: the more you buy, the more you have to dispose of. If you've got extra (e.g., paint), share it with neighbors, friends and family. Try to use it up.
- Use safer substitutes whenever possible.

Dispose of it properly:
- Recycle whenever possible. Used motor oil, car batteries, paint thinners, and some solvents can be refined and reused. Local civic groups can help you identify recycling programs.
- Municipal incineration is a way of dealing with some hazardous wastes. Check with local authorities to see what they accept. Never use incinerators in your home; they don't work.
- Find a licensed contractor or recycling agency. (Look in the yellow pages.) If there's none in your area: call the local wastewater treatment plant for info on disposing of liquid waste, the local sanitation department for info on disposing of solid wastes.
- Participate in a local professional collection program. Many communities do not yet provide this kind of service. If there's none in your community, contact local civic leaders and officials with suggestions for a program. Many of the best collection programs in the country today began with one concerned citizen.

RESOURCES;
Water Pollution Control Federation, 601 Wythe Street, Alexandria, VA 22314-1994, (703) 684-2438. *Call or write for their Household Hazardous Waste Chart.*

Call the EPA hotline—(800)-424-9346—to find out who to contact in your state about household hazardous waste pick-up.

Hazards Management Institute, 10 Newmarket Road, P.O. Box 932, Durham, N.H. 03824

42. CARPOOL TO WORK

In one year, traffic congestion alone wasted 3 billion gallons of gasoline—about 5% of the nation's annual gas consumption.

B ACKGROUND. The growing number of cars on the road pose an enormous threat to the environment. Yet there are few alternatives to driving; in most areas of the U.S., mass transit is woefully inadequate.

So if you're interested in cutting back your driving, you may have to take matters into your own hands. Thus far, the best solution is carpooling.

Carpooling is especially practical if you commute to an urban area. But you can share a ride to work no matter where you live. Even carpooling 8 miles from, say, rural East Calais to Montpelier, Vermont, will save about 2,500 auto miles *per person* every year.

DID YOU KNOW
• One-third of all private auto mileage is racked up commuting to and from work.

• The average commuter car carries only 1.3 riders.

• If each commuter car carried just one more person, we'd save 600,000 gallons of gasoline a day and would prevent 12 million pounds of carbon dioxide from polluting the atmosphere.

• The federal government has cut funding for mass transit by 32%—which makes carpooling even more important.

SIMPLE THINGS TO DO
• Find out how to connect with other commuters. There's no national clearinghouse for carpool information, but many local governments are pushing carpools and can help direct you to the right sources.

• In some places, informal but systematic carpooling arrangements have sprung up near bus or train stops. People line up and commuters stop to fill up their cars, taking advantage of special full-passenger lanes on toll bridges and freeways.

• Advertise carpooling on community bulletin boards (radio and TV stations have them as public services), or in weekly "shoppers."

FOR THE

COMMITTED

43. TRY COMPOSTING

According to Citizens for a Better Environment, between 15-20% of the total municipal waste stream is organic material. All of these materials are very bulky, quickly using up valuable landfill space.

B ACKGROUND. Composting is the process of turning organic material you normally throw away—from grass clippings to apple cores—into a rich fertilizer.

This doesn't mean that you just throw fresh kitchen garbage directly onto the soil: You toss your organic garbage into a specially constructed receptacle, and then you have to maintain it.

How it works: In a compost heap, billions of organisms break the organic wastes down into the forms that can be best used by plants. The finished compost will add nutrients and humus to the soil, improving its texture and increasing its ability to hold air and water.

Besides being a source of natural fertilizer, composting helps cut down the amount of solid waste being dumped in crowded landfills. And we need the relief!

DID YOU KNOW
- Every year we throw away 24 million tons of leaves and grass.
- Leaves alone can account for 75% of the solid waste in the fall.
- The average American family produces more than 1,200 pounds of organic garbage every year.
- About 70% of the garbage Americans create is compostable, including yard waste, food waste, wood, and paper.
- It costs at least $65 per ton to dump solid waste in landfill; the average cost of municipal composting is only $35 per ton.
- **Success Stories:** Composting, combined with curbside collection of recyclables, has allowed towns like Davis, California to cut their garbage in half. In New Jersey, state-sponsored economic incentives have spurred 80 towns to develop composting programs.

SIMPLE THINGS TO DO
Start your own compost pile: The simplest way is to just pile leaves, grass clippings, and weeds in a corner of your garden.

Don't forget: Aluminum foil is recyclable.

This isn't ideal as composting goes, and it takes up a lot of room.... But the clippings will decompose, and won't use landfill space.

A more sophisticated compost pile involves more effort. You'll need to:
• Sort your garbage to separate the organics from the rest.
• Build or buy a small enclosure in which to create the compost.
• Learn how to stack and layer the compost.
• Turn it occasionally to avoid odors and allow the air to circulate.

It's a lot simpler than it might sound. But since we haven't got space to explain it in detail, a good way to start is to send a self-addressed envelope to The Berkeley Ecology Center, 2530 San Pablo Ave., Berkeley, CA. 94702, and ask them for their "Composting" fact sheet. It has the right info to get you going, and answers basic questions.

If you have a yard but no garden:
• Composting is still worthwhile. Donate your compost to friends who garden; they'll appreciate it.

• If you want to recycle your organic garbage without bothering to keep a compost pile, you can participate in community composting projects. These usually involve leaf collection, either curbside or at a centralized composting facility. Call your city government to find out if you've got a composting program in your community. Over 500 communities do, and more are in the planning stages.

• Look for a commercial composter in the yellow pages.

SOURCES:

"Home Composting," a concise how-to brochure, is available for $2.50 plus a SASE with 50 cents postage from Seattle Tilth Association, 4649 Sunnyside Ave., No., Seattle, Washington 98103.

For more detailed information, try:
• *The Rodale Guide to Composting*, by J. Minnich (Rodale Press, 1979).
• *Worms Eat My Garbage*, by M. Appelhoff (Flower Press, 1982).

Astonishing water fact: To produce one steak, 2,607 gallons of water is needed.

44. INSTALL A GRAYWATER TANK

Graywater reuse can cut water consumption by 30%
for the average family of four.

BACKGROUND. Wouldn't it be nice if you could save and reuse the water that goes down the drain in your shower or sink? You can, but it isn't easy. It can be collected in a tank under your house, then siphoned off and used to water your lawn and garden. The water is called "graywater" (for obvious reasons). A graywater tank isn't for everybody; but it if you live in a climate that's constantly plagued by drought and you're an avid gardener, this may be a viable option—you can still have your garden without using more than your share of water.

DID YOU KNOW
• Graywater makes up 60-65% of the total indoor water consumption in an average American home.

• Not all graywater is suitable for reuse—kitchen grease, for instance, needs to be kept out of any graywater recycling system—but much of it is not only as good for plants as clear water, but actually helps some plants thrive.

• Graywater reuse is technically illegal in many states. However, in times of drought, many localities have the latitude to authorize "appropriate" conservation methods; graywater reuse is among them..

• Graywater systems are not for the uncommitted. Setting up a system requires some work and some expense—$200-400 for a basic system built with new parts; $100-200 more if you need a sump pump; labor costs if you hire someone to install it.

SOURCES
Edible Publications, P.O. Box 1841, Santa Rosa, CA 95402
Their excellent booklet, "Graywater Use in the Landscape," provides a concise yet comprehensive discussion of the value and practical considerations of installing and operating a graywater system. Read it before you seriously consider altering your existing plumbing for a graywater tank. Cost: $6 ppd. (CA residents add $0.36 tax).

It takes 100 times more water to produce a pound of meat than a pound of wheat.

45. DRIVE LESS

"Cars are multiplying faster than people. They're outbreathing us, too. They're using up our land area. They're using up our economic strength."—Ernest Callenbach, *author of* Ecotopia.

BACKGROUND. Our entire society is built around having—and driving—cars....So it probably seems like we're suggesting the impossible when we propose a cutback in driving. But other societies have done it: In the Netherlands, for example, 80% of train commuters get to the station on a bicycle; in Denmark, about 30% of all trips are taken on bikes; and Japan even has bicycle parking garages in urban areas.

Whenever Americans complain about the shoddy environmental practices of other cultures (e.g., Brazil rainforest policies), people point out that we own most of the world's vehicles, and we're doing little to control them. They're right. So for the truly committed, this is a priority.

DID YOU KNOW
• On an average, the 140 million cars in America are estimated to travel almost 4 billion miles a day...and according to the DOT, they use over 200 million gallons of gas doing it.
• The ecological effects are staggering. One result of burning 200 million gallons of gas, for example, is the emission of about 4 billion pounds of carbon dioxide into the atmosphere. And that's just one day's worth.

SIMPLE THINGS TO DO
For starters, we could try using an alternative means of transportation—buses, subways, trains, bicycle, or walking—just one day a week. Even that may be tough—but it's worth the effort.

RESULTS
If only 1% of the car owners in America left their cars idle for one day a week, it would save an estimated 42 million gallons of gas a year. Destructive emissions would be cut down commensurately; we'd keep some 840 million pounds of CO_2 out of the atmosphere, for instance.

Every year in the U.S. we lose 7 billion tons of topsoil—an area the size of Connecticut.

46. EAT LOW ON THE FOOD CHAIN

According to Diet for a New America, *over a billion people could be fed by the grain and soybeans eaten by U.S. livestock every year.*

BACKGROUND. We don't think anyone should tell you what to eat—that's too personal. But we do think you should know some facts about how your diet affects the environment. A lot of Americans probably never consider the resources that it takes to put—for example—hamburgers on their dinner tables. We've been blessed with a plentiful food supply; perhaps it's time we tried to conserve the natural resources that support it.

DID YOU KNOW
• According to *Diet for a New America*: If Americans reduced their meat intake by just 10%, the savings in grains and soybeans could adequately feed 60 million people—the number of people who starve to death, worldwide, each year.

• To produce 1 lb. of beef, we need 16 lbs. of grain and soybeans, 2500 gallons of water, and the energy equivalent of one gallon of gasoline.

• Livestock production accounts for more than half of all the water consumed (for all purposes) in the U.S.

• Believe it or not, cows may be contributing to the greenhouse effect. According to one estimate, the world's 1.3 billion cows annually produce nearly 100 million tons of methane—a powerful "greenhouse gas" which, molecule for molecule, traps 25 times as much solar heat as CO_2.

• 220 million acres of land in the U.S. have been deforested for livestock production. 25 million acres (an area the size of Austria) in Brazil, and half the forests in Central America, have been cleared for beef production.

• A third of the surface of North America is devoted to grazing. Half of American croplands grow livestock feed (mostly for cattle).

The hamburgers that McDonald's serves in a week equal more than 16,000 head of cattle.

person who eats meat.

• The value of raw materials consumed to produce food from livestock is greater than the value of all oil, gas and coal consumed in America.

• Growing grains, vegetables and fruits uses less than 5% as much raw materials as does meat production.

SIMPLE THINGS TO DO

• The simplest thing—even if you're a confirmed meat-eater—is to cut down on the amount of beef you eat.

• Experiment with occasional vegetarian meals. There are lots of excellent vegetarian-cuisine cookbooks available.

• Have you tried your hand at edible gardening? Gardening is the #1 recreational pursuit in America. You'll be amazed at how much you can grow in even a tiny plot. Herbs, leafy greens, fruits and even corn can be grown quite handily in most urban settings.

• Support local "farmers' markets." Locally-grown produce is typically fresher, cheaper, and less laden with pesticide residues than produce shipped long distances.

RESOURCES:

•*Diet for a New America*, by John Robbins (Stillpoint Press) *An exhaustive study of the perils of "our addiction to meat," from the waste of natural resources to the health hazards of the American diet to the cruelty to animals.*

• *Diet for a Small Planet*, Frances Moore Lappe´(Ballantine Books). *A revolutionary vegetarian cookbook.*

• *The Moosewood Cookbook*, by Mollie Katzen (Ten Speed Press). *One of the most popular vegetarian cookbooks ever published.*

Astonishing water fact: To produce one serving of chicken, 408 gallons of water is required.

47. START A RECYCLING PROGRAM

*Connecticut, Rhode Island, New Jersey, and Oregon have
all passed legislation that either encourages or
requires recycling by residents.*

B ACKGROUND. We hope, by now, you're excited about recycling. But what happens if you look around your area and discover that there's no recycling program in which to participate.

After talking with professionals who specialize in recycling, our recommendation is that you contact communities where recycling has been tried...and has worked.

RECYCLING SUCCESS STORIES
• "In Rockford, Illinois, residents can win more than $1000 for just taking out the trash. In one of the country's most innovative programs for recycling, Rockford's 'trash lottery' rewards randomly selected households for separating the recyclable materials from their garbage, and pays them from the city's savings in landfill costs."

• "In King County, Washington strong support for recycling brought a postponement of plans to incinerate waste."

• "The metropolitan Portland (Oregon) area has set an ambitious goal. Although the 1.2 million residents already recycle 22% of their wastes, one of the highest rates in the United States, the regional government thinks they can do better. By 1989, Portland must cut its waste by 52%."

• "In Philadelphia, where waste disposal costs increased by 20%, or $11 million, during a one-year period, Mayor Wilson Goode signed curbside recycling legislation into effect in June, 1987."

SOURCES
Environmental Defense Fund, 1616 P St. NW, Washington, D.C. 20036. *Write for their book*, Coming Full Circle. *It's a good way to approach setting up a recycling program. Looks at the issue form all angles, and gives examples of successful programs.Cost: $10.*

48. XERISCAPE

*Native plants need only about half as much
water as imported varieties.*

BACKGROUND. Xeriscape (from the Greek word *Xeros*, meaning *dry*) is a modern approach to landscaping which has become popular due to water shortages. Some years ago, experts realized that much of the water used in residential planting went to plants that were not suited for the regions in which they were being grown. Tests done with equally attractive native varieties showed that it was possible to save as much as 54% of the water, keep plants healthier, and improve soil conditions. Xeriscape is not only practical, it's eminently satisfying—because you'll wind up with an aesthetically pleasing yard that's also ecologically sound.

DID YOU KNOW
• Drought-resistant plants aren't just limited to cacti and succulants. They include hundreds of species of colorful flowers, flowering shrubs, vines and ground covers that provide beautiful alternatives to traditional landscapes. For instance, jasmine, bougainvillea, wisteria, sweet alyssum and daffodil are all low-water use plants.

• There are many low-maintainance grasses, too. In Texas, for instance, where water can be scarce, the standard Bluegrass needs to be watered every four days. Buffalograss, better adapted to the climate, requires water only every 2 - 3 weeks.

SIMPLE THINGS TO DO
• We're not suggesting you go out, rip up your front lawn, and instantly replace it with cactus. We are suggesting you take a new look at landscaping your home. Some of the principles of Xeriscape —drip irrigation, heavy mulching of planting beds, organic soil improvements to allow for better water absorption and retention—are applicable to any garden design.
• Contact a local horticulture society or nursery to learn more.

SOURCES
The Texas Water Development Board, P.O. Box 13231, Capitol Station, Austin, TX 78711. *Write for Xeriscape brochures.*

Growing wildflowers and herbs will provide food for beneficial insects.

49. STAY INVOLVED

B ACKGROUND. Some activists worry that books like this one will lull people into believing that a doing a few positive things for the environment is enough.

It isn't. As we said at the beginning of this book, our "50 Simple Things" are just a start. By making them simple and accessible, we're trying to make it easier for you to get involved.

Now it's up to you to *stay* involved.

There are many ways to do it; one is to work with existing organizations. Here's a list of some we've worked with. Pick a few, and write to them for more information about what you can do.

THE WRITE STUFF

Center for Marine Conservation, 1725 DeSales St. NW, Washington, D.C. 20036

Citizen's Clearinghouse for Hazardous Waste, P.O. Box 926, Arlington, VA 22216

Citizens for a Better Environment, 33 East Congress, Suite 523, Chicago, IL 60605

Earth Island Institute, 300 Broadway, Suite 28, San Francisco, CA 94133

Environmental Action. 1525 New Hampshire NW, Washington, D.C. 20036.

Environmental Defense Fund, 1616 P St. NW, Suite 150, Washington, D.C. 20036

Environmental Policy Institute, 218 D St. SE, Washington, D.C. 20003

Greenhouse Crisis Foundation, 1130 17th St. NW, Suite 630, Washington D.C. 20036

Greenpeace, 1436 U St. NW, Washington, D.C. 20009

Packaging Mania: About 40% of America's aluminum is used for packaging.

Isaak Walton League, 1701 North Fort Myer Dr., #1100, Arlington, VA 22209

National Audubon Society, 645 Pennsylvania Ave SE, Washington D.C. 20003

National Coalition Against the Misuse of Pesticides, 530 7th St. SE, Washington, D.C. 20003

National Wildlife Federation, 1412 16th St. NW, Washington, D.C. 20036

Natural Resources Defense Council, 40 West 20th St., New York, NY 10011

Nature Conservancy International, 1800 North Kent St., Suite 800, Arlington, VA 22209

Oceanic Society, 218 D St. SE, Washington, D.C. 20003

Rainforest Action Network, 300 Broadway, Suite 28, San Francisco, CA 94133

Renew America, 1001 Connecticut Ave. NW, Suite 1719, Washington, D.C. 20036

Rocky Mountain Institute, 1739, Snowmass Creek Road, Snowmass, Colorado 81654

Sierra Club, 730 Polk St., San Francisco, CA 94009

Wilderness Society, 1400 I St. NW, Washington, D.C. 20005

World Resources Institute, 1735 New York Ave. NW, Washington, D.C. 20006

World Wildlife Fund, 1250 24th St. NW, Washington, D.C. 20037

Worldwatch Institute, 1776 Massachusetts Ave. NW, Washington, DC 20036

"When the well is dry, we know the worth of water." —*Poor Richard's Almanack*

50. SPREAD THE WORD

Now that you've invested time reading this book and experimenting with the projects in it, you're aware of some of the ways that one person can make a difference.

Here's another one: Pass the book on to other people...or just pass on what you've learned.

The 1990s should be a very exciting time, with people joining together to protect the most important asset we have—our environment. But in a powerful way, the ability to make this happen begins with you. Friends and family who see that you take environmental problems—and your role in solving them—seriously will show respect...and curiosity. Then they'll listen as you pass on your knowledge and commitment.

It has a cumulative effect. As you inspire them, they'll inspire others. Our ability to have a positive impact will grow proportionately.

We owe it to ourselves and our children to do whatever we can.
Keep it going. We need you.

WRITE TO US
If you've got some ideas
you'd like to pass on, we'd like
to hear them. We'll pass them on, too.

Write to:
THE EARTHWORKS GROUP
Box 25
1400 Shattuck Avenue
Berkeley, CA 94709